J. D. Salinger's

The Catcher in the Rye

Text by
Robert S. Holzman
(M.Ed., Xavier University)
Middletown City Schools
Middletown, Ohio

Gary L. Perkins
(M.S., Miami University of Ohio)
Middletown City Schools
Middletown, Ohio

Illustrations by
Karen Pica

Research & Education Association

Dr. M. Fogiel, Director

MAXnotes® for
THE CATCHER IN THE RYE

Printed in the United States of America

Library of Congress Catalog Card Number 99-75136

International Standard Book Number 0-87891-752-7

MAXnotes® is a registered trademark of Research & Education Association, Piscataway, New Jersey 08854

What **MAXnotes**® *Will Do for You*

This book is intended to help you absorb the essential contents and features of J.D. Salinger's *The Catcher in the Rye* and to help you gain a thorough understanding of the work. Our book has been designed to do this more quickly and effectively than any other study guide.

For best results, this **MAXnotes** book should be used as a companion to the actual work, not instead of it. The interaction between the two will greatly benefit you.

To help you in your studies, this book presents the most up-to-date interpretations of every section of the actual work, followed by questions and fully explained answers that will enable you to analyze the material critically. The questions also will help you to test your understanding of the work and will prepare you for discussions and exams.

Meaningful illustrations are included to further enhance your understanding and enjoyment of the literary work. The illustrations are designed to place you into the mood and spirit of the work's settings.

The **MAXnotes** also include summaries, character lists, explanations of plot, and section-by-section analyses. A biography of the author and discussion of the work's historical context will help you put this literary piece into the proper framework of what is taking place.

The use of this study guide will save you the hours of preparation time that would ordinarily be required to arrive at a complete grasp of this work of literature. You will be well-prepared for classroom discussions, homework, and exams. The guidelines that are included for writing papers and reports on various topics will prepare you for any added work which may be assigned.

The **MAXnotes** will take your grades "to the max."

Dr. Max Fogiel
Program Director

Contents

> **Each chapter includes List of Characters, Summary,
> Analysis, Study Questions and Answers, and
> Suggested Essay Topics.**

MAXnotes® are simply the best – but don't just take our word for it...

"... I have told every bookstore in the area to carry your MAXnotes. They are the only notes I recommend to my students. There is no comparison between MAXnotes and all other notes ..."
    – *High School Teacher & Reading Specialist,*
    Arlington High School, Arlington, MA

"... I discovered the MAXnotes when a friend loaned me her copy of the *MAXnotes for Romeo and Juliet*. The book really helped me understand the story. Please send me a list of stores in my area that carry the MAXnotes. I would like to use more of them ..."
    – *Student, San Marino, CA*

A Glance at Some of the Characters

Holden Caulfield

Mr. Spencer

Mrs. Morrow

Jane Gallagher

Mr. Ossenburger

Ward Stradlater

Sunny

Phoebe

SECTION ONE

Introduction

The Life and Work of J. D. Salinger

Although the known facts of his life are sparse and undramatic, J. D. Salinger's influence on American youth since the 1950s has been profound. More than 40 years after the publication of *The Catcher in the Rye*, students are still sharing it with each other. This is remarkable, considering that there is scant mention of Salinger in current high school anthologies of American literature.

Young people find that he speaks to them with genuine understanding, as they grapple with the contradictions and mixed messages in society today. Moreover, his insights into the human condition, as experienced by adolescents, are just as valid for adults as they, too, cope with life in all of its complexities and compromises. Robert Coles, the prominent Harvard psychiatrist and literary essayist, describes Salinger as "an original and gifted writer, a marvelous entertainer, a man free of the slogans and clichés the rest of us fall prey to."

J. D. (Jerome David) Salinger was born in New York City in 1919 to a Jewish father and a Scotch-Irish mother. There were two children: an older sister and himself. He was asked to leave several preparatory schools because of poor grades before finally graduating from Valley Forge Military Academy in 1936. Although he did not complete a degree, he attended several colleges. These included Columbia University, where he enrolled in a writing course taught by Whit Burnett, a well-respected teacher of young writers.

Salinger was first published in *Story* (1940), a highly regarded periodical established by Whit Burnett. In time, his short stories were published in *Collier's, The Saturday Evening Post, Esquire*, and finally, *The New Yorker*, the magazine for which he wrote almost exclusively after 1948.

Salinger was drafted into the military in 1942 and was transferred to the Counter-Intelligence Corps in 1943. The following year he trained in England, joined the American Army's Fourth Division, and landed at Utah Beach on D-Day. He then served in five European campaigns as Security Agent for the Twelfth Infantry Regiment.

Upon discharge from the army, Salinger returned to live with his parents in New York City. There followed a series of short stories until the publication of *The Catcher in the Rye* in 1951. The book was an instant best seller. His picture appeared on the cover of *Time* magazine, and he became a hero of college students across the country.

But Salinger did not find fame agreeable. With the success of *The Catcher in the Rye*, he moved out of New York City to Tarrytown, New York, then to Westport, Connecticut, and finally, in 1953, to Cornish, New Hampshire. From this point on, he avoided the public eye whenever possible.

Notwithstanding his reclusiveness, he met British-born Clair Douglas, who became his wife in 1955. There were two children during this marriage, a girl and a boy. The marriage ended in divorce in 1967.

Salinger's output, following the success of *The Catcher in the Rye*, has been modest. There have been no additional novels published, only short stories. After *Nine Stories* (1953), his next book, *Franny and Zooey*, did not come out until 1961. This work consists of two lengthy short stories which are related and interdependent, concerning a crisis in the life of the youngest member of the fictional Glass family, Franny.

In 1963, Salinger published another Glass family story sequence, *Raise High the Roof Beam, Carpenters* and *Seymour: An Introduction*. Both stories center on the life and tragic death of Seymour Glass, as narrated by his brother Buddy Glass, who is frequently identified as Salinger's alter-ego.

Careful readers of Salinger's work will notice the influence of his interest in Zen Buddhism and Eastern religious literature in general. More and more, he came to view life as a religious quest for meaning. He felt that logic and intellectual discussion cannot lead to truth. Truth, according to Salinger, can be found only in the daily experience of life itself. The influence of Zen Buddhism and Eastern religions is particularly evident in his works after 1951.

While Salinger's fictional characters have been tirelessly analyzed and discussed, the author himself has continued to remain a mystery. Since the publication of *The Catcher in the Rye*, he has avoided contact with the public, aggressively blocking attempts by those wishing to pry into his personal life. In 1987 he even went to court to prevent the publication of an unauthorized biography by Ian Hamilton. In his suit, he argued copyright infringement by Hamilton for quoting from Salinger's private letters. In 1988, however, a revised version of the work was published, entitled *In Search of J. D. Salinger*.

As a result of his passion for privacy, Salinger has steadfastly refused to reveal details about his personal life. Many critics feel, however, that, in his fiction, he draws heavily on his own experiences, thus revealing more about himself than he may intend.

While Salinger's writing is more substantial than the casual reader may observe, his appeal to both young people and adults remains strong. It is these characteristics—substance and popularity—which suggest that Salinger, indeed, may be an enduring figure in American literature.

Historical Background

The period following World War II was a time of hope, change, and puzzlement. Today's youth have come to know this period through television sitcoms (*Happy Days* and *Ozzie and Harriet*), movies (*Rebel Without a Cause*), and early rock 'n' roll music, which is still heard on "oldies" radio stations. Needless to say, these provide a simplistic picture of this complex period (1945-60).

In reality, an estimated 50 million persons had died during the six years of World War II. They died on the battlefield, of starvation, and as a result of genocide. The United States buried its dead along with the rest of the world, but the country emerged from the war intact, even flourishing, from an economic point of view. The "war industries" continued into the postwar years, causing the economy to expand. It was a time of prosperity, unlike any in history.

Whereas the various New Deal programs of the Roosevelt administration had failed to lift the country out of the Depression, the war had energized the national will, sharply expanding employment, productivity, and capital investment. After the war, automobiles and major appliances were suddenly available. Indeed, everybody needed them because, during the war, raw materials had been used for the war effort rather than for "luxuries" like washing machines and refrigerators. Interstate highways and intercontinental airliners made travel easier, cheaper, and, thus, more available to the middle class. Mass-produced tract houses brought home ownership within the reach of the majority of workers. Jobs were plentiful. The American Dream was within the grasp of everyone.

But this is only part of the story. In 1950, America was at war again. This time it was the Korean War. It was also the beginning of the Cold War between the United States and the Soviet Union. Each side competed with the other in building the biggest and most destructive war machine. Senator Joseph McCarthy heightened the fear of a Communist takeover of this country by recklessly accusing people in government and in the entertainment industry of being Communist subversives. Paradoxically, and of equal importance to the American people, was the competition in space exploration which began with the Soviet launching of *Sputnik*.

Sputnik was the name for three satellites launched by the Soviet Union in October and November 1957 and in May 1958. Their purpose was to investigate whether living organisms could survive space conditions. *Sputnik* came as a tremendous shock to the United States, where technology was viewed as an American "exclusive." Suddenly, Russia—the backward, unsophisticated competitor—had outdistanced the West. Reactions in the United States, in some cases, bordered on hysteria. Although the United States launched a satellite, *Explorer I*, in January 1958, it was too late. America was now "number two" in the space race. But who was to blame? The schools become the scapegoat. In order to close the alleged gap between the Soviet and American educational systems, federal dollars were pumped into the schools to improve science and mathematics education. Education became a national priority, not only to win the Cold War, but to reestablish the United States as "Number one".

Most veterans of World War II and Korea were eager to put the war behind them and get on with their lives. Men and women who had never considered the possibility of higher education before the wars were now enrolling in college because of the GI Bill. Other veterans had skills learned in the military which easily transferred to the manufacturing and business world.

African-American veterans came home from World War II to find people of color still walking the streets of America with their heads down and riding at the back of the bus. They asked themselves, "Did we risk our lives so that we could come home to be the porters and janitors of the richest country in the world?" Clearly their answer was no. It was not long before Rosa Parks, in Montgomery, Alabama, refused to go to the back of the bus (1955), and the civil rights movement was born.

Many veterans from the Second World War and Korea would never recover from the physical and mental wounds received in military action. Veterans, as well as others who had experienced the horrors of war, were thinking anew about the meaning of life. Some saw no meaning at all.

In the mid-fifties, a counter-culture emerged, called the Beat Generation (beatniks). Many of the beatniks fought in the Korean War, were disillusioned with the American Dream, and rejected the materialism of the conventional consumer society. The Beat Generation of writers, among them Allen Ginsberg, Jack Kerouac, Gregory Corso, and Lawrence Ferlinghetti, created a literature around an unconventional lifestyle of Zen Buddhism, drugs, jazz, and a heightened respect for the individual over the masses. They felt that the American way of life was too corrupt to be saved.

Salinger, too, was grappling with life's contradictions, perhaps, because of his own war experiences. In his stories, he lamented the emptiness of contemporary culture. He struggled with the conflict between spiritual values and the materialism and selfishness of the times. He mourned the loss of childhood innocence as each person matures and makes compromises with the sinful world. He wrestled with the fact that it is difficult to be in the world without being soiled by the world. Finding genuine love in a society of imperfect men and women is not easy. Salinger was able to articulate the ambiguities in life with which every man and woman must come to terms.

Although Americans were buying automobiles and saving for a house in the suburbs, they worried about the Cold War due to the hostile relationship between the United States and the Soviet Union. But they were also concerned about the meaning of life, the individual's place in society, and which values mattered, especially with the threat of nuclear destruction hanging overhead. Salinger wrote about every person's need for meaning and authenticity. This is the reason that *The Catcher in the Rye* became a best seller.

Master List of Characters

Holden Caulfield—*the protagonist and narrator of the story.*

D. B.— *Holden's brother.*

Selma Thurmer— *the headmaster's daughter.*

Mr. Spencer—*Holden's history teacher at Pencey Prep.*

Robert Tichener—*one of the boys with whom Holden tossed the football "this time in around October."*

Paul Campbell—*one of the boys with whom Holden tossed the football "this time in around October."*

Mr. Zambesi— *the biology teacher at Pencey Prep.*

Mrs. Spencer— *the wife of Mr. Spencer.*

Mr. Haas— *the headmaster at Elkton Hills School.*

Dr. Thurmer— *the headmaster at Pencey Prep.*

Robert Ackley—*the boy who lives in the room next to Holden.*

Herb Gale—*Ackley's roommate.*

Edgar Marsalla—*the student who created a disturbance during a talk by Mr. Ossenburger.*

Mr. Ossenburger—*an alumnus and benefactor of Pencey Prep, after whom the dormitory wing, in which Holden lives, was named.*

Ward Stradlater—*Holden's roommate at Pencey Prep.*

Howie Coyle— *a student and basketball player at Pencey Prep.*

Hartzell—*Holden and Stradlater's English teacher at Pencey Prep.*

Fitzgerald—*a former girlfriend of Stradlater.*

Phyllis Smith—*the girl who was supposed to be Stradlater's date; instead Jane Gallagher is his date.*

Bud Thaw—*Jane Gallagher is Bud Thaw's girlfriend's roommate.*

Jane Gallagher—*a former girlfriend of Holden's who goes on a date with Stradlater.*

Mal Brossard—*a student at Pencey with whom Holden went to Agerstown.*

Allie—*Holden's younger brother who died of leukemia.*

Ed Banky—*the basketball coach at Pencey, owned the car which Stradlater borrowed for his date with Jane Gallagher.*

Mrs. Schmidt—*the janitor's wife at Pencey Prep.*

Ely— *Ackley's roommate.*

Frederick Woodruff—*a student who lives in the dorm, to whom Holden sells his typewriter.*

Mrs. Morrow—*mother of Ernest Morrow, a classmate; the lady whom Holden met on the train.*

Ernest Morrow—*a classmate of Holden's, son of the lady whom he met on the train.*

Rudolf Schmidt—*the name of the janitor at Holden's dorm and the alias Holden used with Mrs. Morrow on the train.*

Harry Fencer—*president of Holden's class at Pencey Prep.*

Phoebe—*Holden's ten-year-old sister.*

Sally Hayes—*a girlfriend with whom Holden went to the play on Sunday afternoon.*

Mrs. Hayes— *Sally's mother.*

Carl Luce—*a student at Columbia, and Holden's student advisor at Whooton School; they met for drinks at the Wicker Bar.*

Faith Cavendish—*a former stripper who would not meet Holden for a drink.*

Eddie (Edmund) Birdsell— *a student at Princeton who gave Faith Cavendish's name and telephone number to Holden.*

Anne Louise Sherman— *a girl whom Holden once dated.*

Bernice—*one of the three girls whom Holden met in the nightclub; the blonde, the good dancer.*

Marty—*one of the girls whom Holden met in the Lavender Room; the poor dancer.*

Laverne—*one of the girls whom Holden met in the Lavender Room.*

Mrs. Caulfield—*Holden's mother.*

Mrs. Cudahy—*Jane Gallagher's mother.*

Mr. Cudahy—*Jane Gallagher's step-father.*

Horwitz—*the cabdriver who takes Holden to Ernie's and who is unable to tell Holden where the ducks from Central Park go in the winter.*

Ernie—*the owner of a nightclub in Greenwich Village and the featured pianist there.*

Lillian Simmons— *a former girlfriend of D. B.'s, whom Holden meets in Ernie's.*

Raymond Goldfarb—*a boy with whom Holden got drunk on scotch in the chapel at the Whooton School.*

Maurice—*the elevator operator who procured the prostitute for Holden.*

Sunny—*the prostitute procured by Maurice.*

Bobby Fallon—*a neighbor and friend of Holden's in Maine several years ago.*

Arthur Childs—*a student at the Whooton School with whom Holden discusses religious issues.*

The Nuns—*nuns whom Holden meets in Grand Central Station.*

Dick Slagle—*a roommate of Holden's at Elkton Hills School.*

Louis Shaney—*Catholic boy whom Holden met at Whooton School.*

Miss Aigletinger—*a former teacher of Holden's who frequently took her class to the Museum of Natural History.*

Gertrude Levine—*Holden's partner when the class went to the Museum of Natural History.*

Harris Macklin—*a roommate of Holden's for a couple of months at Elkton Hills School.*

George something—*an acquaintance of Sally Hayes whom she saw at the play.*

Al Pike—*Jane Gallagher's date at a Fourth of July dance.*

Bob Robinson—*a friend of Holden's, who had an inferiority complex.*

James Castle—*the boy who committed suicide at Elkton Hills School.*

Mr. Antolini—*Holden's former English teacher at Elkton Hills.*

Richard Kinsella—*a classmate of Holden's who digressed a great deal in oral expression class when giving speeches.*

Mr. Vinson—*the teacher of oral expression at Pencey Prep.*

Summary of the Novel

The story covers a three-day period in the life of Holden Caulfield. He has been notified that he has just flunked out of prep school, and he begins his journey home, where he must face his parents. He is also considering whether he should simply go out west and start a new life, rather than go home at all.

Before he leaves Pencey, Ackley, the boy who lives in the next room, comes over to visit. Ackley has several personal habits which make him unappealing, but Holden tolerates him. Stradlater, Holden's roommate, then comes in to freshen up for a date. Although Stradlater is handsome and has the veneer of sincerity, Holden thinks he is a phony. That evening, in New York City, Holden joins three female tourists in a nightclub and gets stuck with the check. Back at his hotel, he accepts an offer from the elevator operator for some female companionship. When the girl arrives, he is depressed by the hollowness of an encounter with a prostitute and tells her that he is not in the mood for sex.

The next day, Sunday, Holden meets two nuns at breakfast. He enjoys their conversation and insists on giving them a contribution. That afternoon, he takes his old girlfriend, Sally, to see a play. Still ambivalent about going home, Holden tries to talk Sally into running away with him. When he insults her, she asks him to leave. Later, he goes home and sneaks into the house to see his sister, Phoebe, before he runs away. After they talk, he decides to spend the night at the home of his former English teacher, Mr. Antolini. Holden suspects that his former teacher is a pervert when he is awakened by Mr. Antolini petting him on the head. Holden makes up a flimsy excuse about getting his bags from the train station and bolts from the apartment. Holden continues to be obsessed by his plan to go out west. On Monday morning, he writes Phoebe a note at her school asking her to meet him near the Metropolitan Museum. Phoebe meets him with suitcase in hand. She has decided to run away with him, but he tells her that he is not going away after all. They visit the zoo, and then Phoebe wants to ride the carousel in the park. Before she gets on, he confirms to her that he really is going home. While standing in a soaking rain, watching Phoebe ride the carousel, he feels so happy that he is on the verge of tears.

The novel is divided into three sections, with the first chapter as an introduction and the last chapter as an epilogue. The first part includes Chapters Two through Seven, covering the period at Pencey Prep. Chapters Eight through Twenty make up the second part, which recounts Holden's wandering about New York, and ends with his decision to go home. Chapters Twenty-one through Twenty-five describe his time with Phoebe. Holden is the narrator of the story which is told as a "flashback."

Estimated Reading Time

The average reader should be able to read the book in four to six hours. The colloquial and engaging style of Holden's narration makes for a quick read. The reading could be broken down into two or three two-hour sittings, though many readers are able, if they have the time, to read the book in one long sitting.

The Catcher in the Rye

Chapter 1

New Characters:

Holden Caulfield: *the narrator of the story*

D.B.: *Holden's brother*

Selma Thurmer: *the headmaster's daughter*

Mr. Spencer: *Holden's history teacher at Pencey Prep*

Robert Tichener: *a student at Pencey Prep*

Paul Campbell: *a student at Pencey Prep*

Mr. Zambesi: *the biology teacher at Pencey Prep*

Mrs. Spencer: *the wife of Mr. Spencer, the history teacher*

Summary

Holden, the narrator, is telling the story from a place in California, near Hollywood. Because he is run down physically, and is probably mentally exhausted as well, it appears that he is in a sanitarium to recover and regain his strength.

His expulsion from prep school has pushed him over the edge. He was failing four subjects and clearly not applying himself. The story begins on Saturday afternoon. He is reflecting on getting ready to leave Pencey Prep. He contrasts the reality of life at Pencey with the advertisements he has seen: a picture of boys playing polo with the caption of the school's mission statement: "to mold boys into splendid, clear-thinking young men." In truth, he says, there is no more molding here than at any other school, and, furthermore, he says, he has never seen a horse near the place.

About three o'clock in the afternoon on Saturday, Holden is watching the football game from up on a hill. It happens that he, as manager of the fencing team, left the foils and other equipment on the subway that morning, and the team was unable to play. He fears that he will be ignored or reviled if he gets close to the other students.

Holden is concerned because he does not *feel* much about leaving, neither sadness nor elation. He is trying to feel something. It's only as he thinks about tossing football with a couple of guys one evening that he begins to feel a kind of vague regret or sadness about leaving.

He observes that few girls go to the games, but is reminded of the fact that Selma Thurmer, the headmaster's daughter, frequently attends. He likes her because she does not pretend that her father is any more than he really is, which, in Holden's opinion, is a phony slob.

The other reason that he is watching the game from afar is that he is on his way to say good-bye to Mr. Spencer, his history teacher. Mr. Spencer had sent him a note that he wanted to see Holden, since he knew that Holden was not coming back to Pencey. He was stopping by the house because Mr. Spencer was sick with the grippe. Mrs. Spencer cordially greets him at the door and invites him in to visit with Mr. Spencer.

Analysis

Holden has a sharp eye for identifying the lack of authenticity in others. The headmaster is "a phony slob." The advertisement for Pencey Prep is a lie. His brother D.B. has sold out to Hollywood for money. In the first chapter, Holden would have the reader believe that only Selma and himself are clearly not phony. Is Holden's eye sharp enough to see himself accurately? One is reminded of the famous line from *Hamlet*, "The lady doth protest too much, me thinks."

Salinger's use of dialect is often compared to Mark Twain's use of dialect in his novels. It is a difficult medium to use, but when it is done well, it is quite effective. The colloquial style and the un-

necessary use of vulgarities present a colorful, vivid picture of a
teenager who is trying to appear "cool" and grown up, but who has
some problems.

In the first chapter, Holden speaks about feelings or the lack
of them. He does not feel anything about leaving Pencey, and this
disturbs him. He tries to conjure up some kind of feeling—any kind
will do. Without feeling, one walks through life without living it.
Knowing and feeling cannot be separated; they are one. Holden
says that you do not know you are doing something unless you
feel it. He finally gets a pleasant feeling about Pencey when he remembers tossing a football one evening with a couple of "nice
guys." Holden finds his "good-bye" in this association with fellow
students. He reaches out to people in an attempt to blot out his
loneliness. This reaching out to others in an attempt to connect
becomes a recurring theme in this book.

Study Questions

1. Who is Holden Caulfield?

2. Who is D.B., and why is Holden somewhat contemptuous
   of him?

3. What is the reality of Pencey Prep in contrast to the advertisements, as seen by Holden?

4. Why does Holden watch the game from the hill?

5. Who is Selma Thurmer, and why did Holden like her?

6. Who is Mr. Spencer, and why was Holden going to visit him?

7. Why was Holden trying to "feel" some kind of good-bye?

8. What does Holden think about the other students who attend Pencey?

9. How popular was the sport of polo at Pencey Prep?

10. Does Holden blame others for his flunking out of school?

Answers

1. Holden Caulfield is the narrator of the story. He has just been
   asked to leave Pencey Prep for failing four subjects. He is

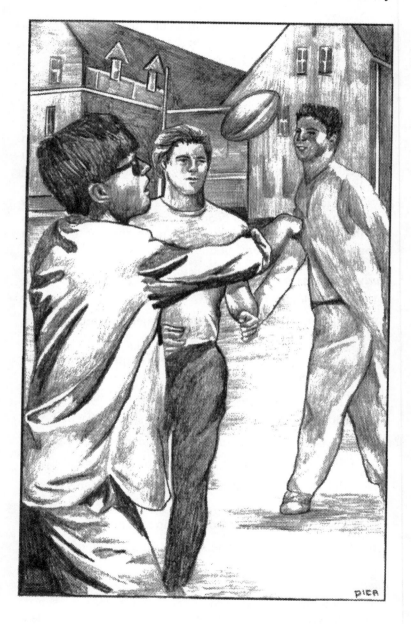

telling the story from California, where he is recuperating from being run-down.

2. D.B. is Holden's older brother, who is a writer. Holden thinks he has prostituted himself because he is in Hollywood writing scripts for movies rather than writing short stories.

3. Holden feels that Pencey has high academic standards, but he is skeptical about its claim to mold boys into "splendid, clear-thinking young men." He thinks that those boys who were splendid and clear thinkers were probably such before they enrolled.

4. He was reluctant to go down to the stands because he feared he would be ignored by the other students, due to his having left the fencing equipment on the subway train the day before. He was the team manager and, because of his error, the team was unable to compete.

5. Selma is the daughter of the headmaster. Although she is not very attractive, Holden likes her because she is not a phony.

6. Mr. Spencer is Holden's history teacher. He had invited Holden to visit him because he knew that Holden was not returning to school after Christmas.

7. Holden is concerned because he did not feel happy or sad about leaving Pencey. He wants to feel something because he says you do not know you are doing something until you feel it.

8. He says that Pencey is full of crooks. The more expensive the school is, the more crooks it has. Yet he did mention that Tichener and Campbell were nice guys.

9. Holden implies that polo was only in the minds of the school publicists. He himself had never seen a horse near the place.

10. Holden readily admits that he did not apply himself, although he had been warned frequently that he was in danger of failing.

Suggested Essay Topics
1. Discuss Holden's obsession with phoniness.
2. Discuss Holden's view of the relationship between knowing and feeling.
3. Discuss Salinger's use of dialect. Compare or contrast Holden's dialect with the dialect of teenagers today.

Chapter 2

New Characters:

Mr. Haas: *the headmaster at Elkton Hills School*

Dr. Thurmer: *the headmaster at Pencey Prep*

Summary
Holden is led into the bedroom by Mrs. Spencer, where Mr. Spencer is sitting in a chair, still not fully recovered from the grippe. Holden liked Mr. Spencer as much, if not more than he liked any adult, and was disappointed to find that he was to be lectured. The tone of the lecture was condescending and included reading aloud from Holden's failing examination paper. Holden was humiliated and disappointed that Mr. Spencer would do this. The lecture was laced with the clichés adults reserve for children when they are scolding them, e.g., how do you feel about flunking out of school? Aren't you concerned about your future? You'll care about your future when it is too late. Holden made an excuse to leave and left rather abruptly. He concludes that Mr. Spencer cares about him, even though it is expressed in an awkward manner.

Analysis
Holden's anecdote about the Navajo blanket suggests that he likes Mr. Spencer about as well as he likes any adult. He was attracted by the humanness of Mr. Spencer's taking delight in a simple thing like an Indian blanket. Despite the fact that Mr. Spencer was old, he still had some appreciation for the little joys in life. Holden, thus, came to visit Mr. Spencer out of affection and respect, as well as duty.

Coming in with these positive feelings, Holden is disappointed to find that he is in for a lecture. Holden is subjected to the typical reaction when an adult does not approve of the behavior of a young person. Spencer's lecture includes the usual, tired clichés: do you blame me for failing you? What would you have done in my place? Why did you do it (flunk out of two previous schools)? Aren't you concerned about your future? You'll care when it's too late. I'd like to put some sense into your head.

Worst of all, Mr. Spencer humiliates Holden by reading aloud from his examination paper. Holden's initial reaction is outrage, bordering on hate. Yet, despite Spencer's cruel behavior, Holden, in the end, tries to be understanding. He feels that, in his own way, Spencer really cares about him. Holden acknowledges this, in his own way, by "sort of put[ting] my hand on his shoulder....Then we shook hands. And all that crap. It made me feel sad as hell, though."

When Mr. Thurmer meets with Holden to discuss the expulsion, he explains that life is a game which should be played according to the rules. Holden cynically agrees, but only if on the winning team. Up to this point, he does not feel like much of a winner. He has been kicked out of three schools now. The fencing team is angry with him. He has no close friends. Most of the people mentioned up to this point, Holden considers "phonies." Thus, life, viewed as a game, does not hold much interest or meaning for him. Moreover, he suspects that there may be more to life than just living it according to other people's rules.

During the discussion with Spencer of whether Holden's parents know of his expulsion, Holden reflects on his inner conflicts between feeling young and old at the same time: sometimes he feels and acts like an adult; at other times, he feels and acts like a child. Although he is only 17, he is over six feet tall and has some gray hair. But he says, "And yet I still act sometimes like I was only about twelve." Every adolescent knows, and most adults can vividly remember, these turbulent and confusing emotions pulling in opposite directions.

Holden's style of narration is very interesting in this chapter— we hear him say one thing to Mr. Spencer, and then follow it up with a scathing sarcastic comment to the opposite effect, directed at the reader. On the one hand, we have the feeling that we are his confidant—that we are getting his "real" attitude toward the scene in these sarcastic comments, as if we are laughing "with him." At the same time, however, for all he has to say about phonies, this might seem to be a "phony" kind of behavior.

Salinger's genius is in using dialect and images which bring to life the characters and the life situations as seen through the eyes of a teenager. Holden's dialect is that of the teenager of the late forties and early fifties. The images are colorful, sensory-laden, and common to the lives of everyone. Consider, for example, the smell of Vicks Nose Drops in a sick room, the ratty, old bathrobe, the bumpy chest and white legs of an old man. Salinger creates a picture that the reader instinctively knows is right.

Study Questions

1. What had Mr. Spencer bought and shown the boys when they were visiting him one Sunday?

2. What advice did Dr. Thurmer give to Holden?

3. Did Holden agree with Dr. Thurmer's description of life as a game? Explain your answer.

4. Was Pencey Prep really the fourth school from which Holden was asked to leave? Explain your answer.

5. What did Holden think about Mr. Spencer's description of his parents as "grand people"?

6. Why did Holden write Mr. Spencer a note at the end of his examination paper?

7. What was Holden thinking about while he said the following: "I told him I was a real moron, and all that stuff. I told him how I would've done exactly the same thing if I'd been in his place, and how most people didn't appreciate how tough it is being a teacher."

8. Why did Holden leave Elkton Hills School?

9. What excuse did Holden give Mr. Spencer for having to end the visit?

10. Holden told Mr. Spencer not to worry about him. What reason did he give for not worrying?

Answers

1. Mr. Spencer had bought a Navajo blanket from an Indian in Yellowstone Park.

2. Dr. Thurmer said that life was a game and should be played according to the rules.

3. Holden felt that life was a game only if you were on the team with all the "hot-shots." But if you were on the other side, i.e., with no hot-shots, then it was not a game.

4. Holden said it was "about the fourth school," but the names of only two other schools are mentioned in the novel: Whooton School and Elkton Hills School.

5. Holden disliked the use of the word "grand." He said that use of it was phony.

6. Holden wrote the note so that Mr. Spencer would not feel badly about flunking him.

7. Holden was thinking about the ducks in Central Park, i.e., where they went when the lagoon froze over.

8. Holden left Elkton Hills School primarily because he was surrounded by phonies.

9. Holden said that he had to go to the gym to pick up equipment in order to take it home with him.

10. Holden said that he was just going through a phase and that everyone goes through phases.

Suggested Essay Topics

1. Discuss Dr. Thurmer's concept of life as a "game." Do you agree with it? Why? Why not?

2. Discuss the relationship between Holden and Mr. Spencer. Is it a personal, caring relationship or simply a professional relationship between teacher and student?

3. Discuss the conflicting teenage emotions of sometimes feeling like a child and sometimes feeling like an adult. Discuss whether teenagers sometimes want to be treated as adults and at other times want to be treated as children.

Chapter 3

New Characters:

Robert Ackley: *the boy who lives in the room next to Holden*

Herb Gale: *Ackley's roommate*

Edgar Marsalla: *the student who created a disturbance during a talk by Mr. Ossenburger*

Mr. Ossenburger: *alumnus and benefactor of Pencey Prep, after whom the dormitory wing, in which Holden lives, was named*

Ward Stradlater: *Holden's roommate at Pencey Prep*

Summary

Holden returns to his room in the Ossenburger Memorial Wing of the dormitory. Ossenburger, an undertaker, is an alumnus and benefactor of Pencey Prep. Mr. Ossenburger spoke to the student body earlier in the year about the role Jesus played in his life. Holden was contemptuous toward Ossenburger because he viewed him as a man who used religion to make more money. When he arrives at his room, Holden decides to read a book, which leads him to a discussion of his favorite authors. Shortly after he began to read, Ackley, a student in the room next door, comes over to visit. Ackley is an unpleasant fellow whose behavior Holden finds annoying. A while later, Stradlater, Holden's roommate, enters the room. Ackley leaves because he does not like Stradlater, whom he thinks is conceited. Stradlater begins changing clothes and preparing for a date with a girl who is waiting for him in the Annex.

Analysis

There are several critical references to phony people and phoniness itself by Holden in the first two chapters. Recall that he refers to the headmaster, Mr. Thurmer, as a phony, and he mentions that he was surrounded by phonies at Elkton Hills. In addition, he makes reference to the advertisement in magazines for Pencey Prep which does not accurately portray the school. Thus, it comes as a surprise to the reader to hear him say that he is "the most terrific liar

you ever saw in your life." He says, in effect, that if someone asks him a question, he is as likely as not to tell a lie. What is the difference between being phony and telling a lie? A phony is presenting oneself as someone he is not; this is very puzzling, indeed. Holden appears to be as phony as the people he rails against. What comes to mind is the Freudian defense mechanism, projection, whereby one projects onto another the traits or shortcomings he sees in himself. Is it possible that Holden accepts in himself the faults which he vehemently denounces in others?

As Holden goes about exercising his self-appointed role of unmasking phoniness, he focuses on Ossenburger, the counterfeit religious philanthropist. Ossenburger proclaims to all that he is a religious man. He thinks of himself as a "buddy" to the Almighty. He falls to his knees often in prayer. But he calls on God only when he needs help—no shyness in him about approaching the throne of God. He uses the Divinity as a lucky charm, the way a child uses a rabbit's foot for good luck. Ossenburger calls on God only when he wants more of life's material goods. His religion is a burlesque of the Gospel, nothing more than a veiled version of selfishness. "I can just see the big phony bastard shifting into first gear and asking Jesus to send him a few more stiffs." Thus, Holden's contempt for Mr. Ossenburger.

Holden flunks out of three schools, refers to himself as illiterate in this chapter, and calls himself a moron when talking to Mr. Spencer in Chapter Two. Yet he seems to boast that he enjoys reading serious literature, e.g., *Out of Africa, Return of the Native, Of Human Bondage*. He claims to have left Elkton Hills because he was surrounded by phonies. Does he really believe this notion? He has been in three schools, has almost no friends, yet wants to have his favorite authors as "terrific" friends whom he could call on the telephone "whenever [he] felt like it." His relationships in fantasy are more real than his relationships in reality. Knowing himself and how he really feels about things is not exactly a strong suit for Holden. Is it possible that Holden does not yet recognize that being authentic is just as difficult for himself as it is for everyone else?

Study Questions

1. Who is Ossenburger?
2. What was the substance of Ossenburger's speech?
3. Who are Holden's favorite authors?
4. How does Holden determine whether a book is outstanding?
5. What does Ackley usually do when he comes to visit Holden?
6. What is it about Ackley that Holden finds annoying?
7. Give an example of something which Ackley considered very funny.
8. Why does Ackley not like Stradlater?
9. What does Holden say in defense of Stradlater?
10. What did Stradlater want to borrow from Holden?

Answers

1. Ossenburger is the wealthy undertaker for whom a dormitory wing at Pencey Prep was named.

2. Ossenburger said that when he was in trouble he prayed to God. In addition, Jesus should be thought of as one's buddy.

3. Holden's favorite authors are his brother, D.B., and Ring Lardner.

4. A book is outstanding if, when you are finished reading it, you wish that the author was a good friend, and you could call him on the telephone whenever you felt like it.

5. He usually walks around the room and picks up Holden's personal things from his desk and chiffonier. What is equally irritating to Holden is that he always puts things back in the wrong places, seemingly on purpose.

6. Holden is annoyed by Ackley's poor personal hygiene, his lack of respect for the privacy of others, and his overall thoughtlessness.

7. Ackley thought it was funny when the tennis racket hit Holden on the head.

8. Ackley thinks that Stradlater is conceited and has a superior attitude.

9. Holden says that Stradlater is generous in sharing his clothing.

10. Stradlater wanted to borrow Holden's hound's-tooth jacket.

Suggested Essay Topics

1. Holden says that a book is good, if, when you are finished, you wish the author were a personal friend of yours so you could call him on the telephone whenever you feel like it. What authors do you wish were your personal friends? What would you like to say to them?

2. Holden describes Ossenburger's religion as bogus. Discuss religious beliefs which you feel that Holden would regard as genuine.

Chapter 4

New Characters:

Howie Coyle: *a student and basketball player at Pencey Prep*

Jane Gallagher: *an old friend of Holden's who goes on a date with Stradlater*

Summary

Holden engages in conversation with Stradlater while he prepares for his date. Holden makes a point of describing Stradlater as a person who is excessively concerned about his personal appearance, but, in reality, is a "secret slob." While he is shaving, Stradlater asks Holden to do him a favor: to write a composition for him. He cautions Holden not to make it too good, for fear that the teacher will discover that Stradlater really did not write it. Further discussion reveals that Stadlater's date is an old friend of Holden's. Holden, very animated, begins telling him all about her:

that she is a dancer, likes to play checkers, and had a rough childhood. Stradlater, however, is not interested because he sees Jane as a mere sexual commodity, just another conquest. It suddenly occurs to Holden that Jane is not safe around Stradlater. After Stradlater leaves, Ackley returns to Holden's room. Holden is glad to see him because his presence distracts him from worrying about Jane's well-being.

Analysis

Holden's feelings toward Ackley are characterized by both strong dislike, on the one hand, and a willingness to tolerate him, on the other. Ackley's physical blemishes and personality flaws are clearly visible for all to see—his pimply face, his disgusting personal habits, his unlimited selfishness. But Holden tolerates Ackley because his company, unpleasant as it is, is better than being alone.

On the surface, Ackley and Stradlater are direct opposites. Ackley is unpleasant to look at and be around; Stradlater is good looking and can be very charming. But the truth is: they are very much alike.

Ackley's flaws are manifest. His personal habits and hygiene are repulsive. He savors gossip and enjoys "running down" students whom he does not like, which is just about everyone.

Stradlater's faults are hidden behind a facade of good looks and a smooth tongue. He is indifferent to other people. For example, Stradlater compliments Holden on his new hat, but only because he hopes that flattery will persuade Holden to ghost-write a composition for him. His behavior is transparent to Holden. As Stradlater prepares to go on a date with an old friend of Holden's, Jane Gallagher, Holden goes to great lengths to tell him all about her. But Stradlater is not interested in background information on Jane—not interested until Holden mentions Jane's stepfather running around the house naked in front of her. Finally, Holden asks Stradlater that he not tell Jane that he had flunked out of Pencey Prep. But he knows there is no danger of this because what happens to Holden is not important enough for Stradlater to even remember.

Ackley, Stradlater, and Holden all have difficulties developing and sustaining interpersonal relationships. The truth is that all three have much in common. Ackley can barely get outside of himself. Stradlater only pretends to show interest in others. Holden is hypercritical of almost everyone and seems to have no close friends at all. Each is simply a variation on the theme of human selfishness.

What makes Holden different is that he still seems to care about some people. After the lecture and embarrassment of having his examination paper read aloud, Holden touches Spencer on the shoulder and expresses sadness at having to leave. In the case of Jane, he sees a friend in danger from a smooth predator. He worries about Jane and what might happen to her at the hands of Stradlater.

Study Questions

1. According to Holden, Ackley and Stradlater are both slobs. In what way are they different as slobs?

2. What favor does Stradlater ask of Holden?

3. According to Stradlater, what constitutes a good composition?

4. According to Ackley, what was it about Howie Coyle which made him a good basketball player?

5. What does Holden have to say about Stradlater's sense of humor?

6. What was unique about the way in which Jane Gallagher played checkers?

7. What does Holden say about Jane Gallagher's home life that piqued Stradlater's curiosity?

8. How does Holden know that Stradlater would not tell Jane Gallagher that he had been kicked out of Pencey Prep?

9. When Stradlater asks Holden to write the composition for him, what does he say regarding the level of quality he wants?

10. Why is Holden glad to see Ackley return to his room?

Answers

1. Both are slobs, but Stradlater is a secret slob, who looks good on the outside.

2. Stradlater asks that Holden write a composition for him.

3. A good composition, according to Stradlater, is one which has all the punctuation in the right places.

4. Ackley felt that being a good basketball player was simply a question of having a perfect build for basketball.

5. Holden says that Stradlater does not have too bad a sense of humor because he laughed at Holden's tap dancing.

6. When Jane Gallagher played checkers, she never moved any of her kings. She kept them all in the back row.

7. Holden says that Jane's stepfather used to run around the house naked in front of her.

8. Stradlater does not care enough about Holden's predicament to even bother to mention it to Jane Gallagher.

9. Stradlater tells Holden not to work too hard on the composition or make it too good. It is necessary only that it be very descriptive.

10. Holden is glad to see Ackley because his presence distracts Holden from worrying about Jane Gallagher.

Suggested Essay Topics

1. According to Stradlater, good writing is simply a question of getting the commas in the right places. What do you think are some characteristics of good writing?

2. Discuss the extent to which Holden's ability to develop and maintain interpersonal relationships is better than Ackley's and Stradlater's.

Chapter 5

New Characters:

Mal Brossard: *a friend of Holden's who is on the wrestling team and with whom Holden goes into Agerstown*

Allie: *Holden's younger brother who died of leukemia*

Summary

After the Saturday night steak dinner at Pencey, Holden makes plans to go to the movies with Mal Brossard and asks Ackley to join them. It happens that both Mal and Ackley have seen the movie, so they have hamburgers, play the pinball machine, and return to the dorm by 8:45 p.m. Brossard goes to look for a bridge game and Ackley comes into Holden's room and discusses his sexual exploits, which Holden has heard before. Finally, Holden asks him to leave and begins writing the composition for Stradlater. Rather than writing a description of a room or a house, Holden writes a description of his younger brother Allie's baseball glove. Allie died of leukemia in 1946 when the family was in Maine. Allie has written poetry all over the glove so he has something to read when he gets bored in the outfield. Holden was very fond of his brother and discusses his reaction to Allie's death. As he finishes the essay, Holden can hear Ackley snoring and comments that one has to feel sorry for Ackley when one considers all the problems he has.

Analysis

Holden finds himself unable to resist pointing out phoniness wherever he sees it. Of course, he is always looking for it outside of himself. He opens the chapter by observing how Pencey Prep serves steak on Saturday nights as a way of suggesting that high quality characterizes all aspects of the school. He has a tendency to attribute a less than noble motive for an action wherever possible. For example, he did it with Pencey's magazine advertisement, and he did it when he described Ossenburger. Less than noble motives drive everyone except himself—he thinks.

In Chapter Two, during his visit with Spencer, Holden says, "People always think something's all true." In Chapter Five, Holden

betrays the fact that he is not one of these people. He has many inconsistencies and clearly does not see life only in blacks and whites. For example, movies have been a target for him since the second page of the novel when he criticized his brother, D.B., for writing movie scripts. Yet there have been several allusions to movies, e.g., the tap dancing scene, which suggests that he has been to many movies, and the fact that he is intending to go to a movie that evening. Also, after being so critical of Ackley's annoying behaviors in Chapter Four, he invites him to go to the movies with him because Ackley "never did anything on Saturday night...."

In Chapter One, Holden has difficulty coming up with memories of Pencey Prep. He was concerned that he had no feelings about the place as he was leaving. Yet in this chapter he refers to Mal Brossard as a friend and talks about the enjoyable snowball fight in the beautiful snow after dinner. Almost in spite of himself, Holden seems to have some pleasant memories of Pencey Prep.

What do all these inconsistencies mean? Does Holden not understand himself at all? Or, is he just like the rest of us, in that we see the world differently, depending on whether we are looking at the cloud or the silver lining, whether the glass is half-full or half-empty. Is this being phony or simply being human?

Allie is only the second person introduced so far about whom Holden expresses unmitigated affection. The other person is Jane Gallagher. There is some evidence beginning to build which suggests that Holden likes only those with whom he does not have to interact or engage in relationship. He has no real contact with Allie because he is dead. Allie is a memory. Holden kept Jane Gallagher from being real by refusing to go to the Annex and talk to her. She too is only a memory.

Study Questions

1. In Holden's opinion why does Pencey Prep serve steak on Saturday night?

2. What is Ackley's characteristic response whenever he is asked to go somewhere with the other boys?

3. Why do Holden, Brossard, and Ackley not go to the movies after all?

4. Why does Holden not like to sit next to Brossard and Ackley at the movies?
5. What card game does Brossard enjoy most of all?
6. What does Holden write about for Stradlater's composition?
7. Why did Allie have writing on his baseball mitt?
8. How did Allie die?
9. How did Holden react to Allie's death?
10. Does Holden express dislike or sympathy for Ackley at the end of this chapter?

Answers

1. Holden thinks that steak is served on Saturday so that when parents who visit on Sunday ask what was served last night, the boys would answer, "Steak."
2. Ackley's usual response is never to answer right away. Then he asks who else is going.
3. They do not go to the movie because Brossard and Ackley had already seen the movie that was playing.
4. Brossard and Ackley laugh excessively while watching a movie.
5. Brossard enjoys playing bridge.
6. Holden writes about his brother Allie's baseball mitt.
7. Allie had poems written on the mitt so that he would have something to read when he was in the field, and nobody was up at bat.
8. Allie died of leukemia on July 18, 1946.
9. Holden slept in the garage the night Allie died and broke all the windows in the garage with his fist.
10. Holden catalogs all of Ackley's physical problems and concludes that one had to feel sorry for him.

Suggested Essay Topics

1. Describe your understanding of Holden's relationship to Allie and Jane Gallagher.

2. Given Holden's exceptional writing ability, why do you suppose he did not dash off a simple descriptive composition rather than going to the trouble of writing an essay about his brother's baseball glove? Discuss your answer.

Chapter 6

New Characters:

Ed Banky: *the basketball coach at Pencey; owned the car which Stradlater borrowed for his date with Jane Gallagher*

Mrs. Schmidt: *the janitor's wife*

Summary

Holden has been worried all evening that Stradlater would take advantage of Jane while on their date. By the time Stradlater returns, Holden is furious with him. Holden is made even angrier when Stradlater does not like the essay which Holden had written for him. Holden immediately tears it up and throws it away.

Holden, not very discreetly, tries to find out what happened on the date. When Stradlater sarcastically indicates that what transpired is privileged information, Holden hits Stradlater, and a fight ensues. Holden, his face bloody and clearly defeated, admits that he really is not much of a fighter. The chapter ends with Holden going over to see Ackley.

Analysis

Holden is consumed with worry over Jane Gallagher. He expresses contempt for Stradlater and the way that he treats women. Holden feels very protective of her, almost chivalrous. What is implied, however, is that Jane Gallagher is unable to take care of herself—not a politically correct idea in our age of gender equality. This gallant attitude toward women is more characteristic of the fifties than of our own day. The Women's Liberation movement

was begun symbolically with the publication of Betty Freidan's book, *The Feminine Mystique*. But this was not written until 1963. It is curious that Holden characterizes Stradlater as a person who tried to keep all the rules. In a sense, Stradlater is attempting to maintain this pretense of being upright and honorable: to appear to do the right thing is as good as doing the right thing. Or, as is often said today: perception is reality. Thus, he did not keep the rules from principle, but only for the sake of appearances. He had no compunction about borrowing Ed Banky's car for the date even though it was forbidden by school rules. He had no scruples about asking Holden to write a composition for him. His only concern was that it not be too good, so he would not get caught.

In the fight between Holden and Stradlater, Stradlater's only concern is that Holden stop questioning him about the date. It is as if Holden can think ill of Stradlater, but he should not express those thoughts aloud. It offends the notion of a good appearance when Holden expresses what Stradlater is really like inside. Stradlater does not want to look at himself as he really is. Stradlater does not defend himself against the accusations. He simply does not want to hear these truths expressed. Moreover, Holden calls him a moron because morons will not discuss problems intelligently. They pretend that problems do not exist. One wonders whether Holden is a "closet" moron because he would not discuss his faults intelligently with Spencer. He made up excuses as to why he was kicked out of previous schools and would not explain why he was failing at Pencey Prep.

Holden has gone to great lengths to explain Ackley's shortcomings and offensive behaviors. Yet, he goes directly to Ackley's room after the fight. He even mentions how the room stinks because of Ackley's disagreeable personal habits, but it is clear that he has come to Ackley for comfort.

Study Questions

1. Why is Holden so interested in what happened on Stradlater's date?

2. Why does Stradlater not like the composition which Holden wrote for him?

3. Why does Holden smoke in bed?

4. Where did Stradlater go on his date with Jane Gallagher?
5. How would you describe Holden's attitude toward athletes?
6. Why does Holden punch Stradlater?
7. According to Holden, how can you identify a moron?
8. Why is Stradlater nervous after hitting Holden?
9. What does Holden do before looking in the mirror?
10. What is Holden's reaction to all the blood?

Answers

1. Holden is concerned that Stradlater may take advantage of Jane Gallagher.

2. Stradlater's understanding is that the essay should be a description of a room or a house. Holden wrote a description of his brother's baseball glove.

3. Holden smokes in bed because it irritates Stradlater.

4. Stradlater says that he spent the evening in the car with Jane.

5. Holden sees athletes as a clique which is dispensed from following the rules.

6. Holden punches Stradlater because he assumes that Stradlater had seduced Jane on their date.

7. Holden says that a moron can be recognized in that he never wants to discuss anything intelligently.

8. Stradlater fears that he may have seriously injured Holden.

9. Holden first puts on his hunting cap.

10. Holden says that he is partly scared and partly fascinated by the blood. Also, he feels that it makes him look tough.

Suggested Essay Topics

1. Why do you think Holden agrees to write a composition for Stradlater?

2. Why do you think Stradlater feels compelled to follow the rules?

Chapter 7

New Characters:

Ely: *Ackley's roommate*

Frederick Woodruff: *a student, who lives in the dorm, to whom Holden sells his typewriter*

Summary

After the fight with Stradlater, Holden goes to Ackley's room looking for comfort, but finds none. Ackley's only concern is to learn the reasons for the fight. When Holden asks to sleep in Ely's bed, Ackley is unwilling to give permission because Ely might come back that evening. The truth is that Ely goes home every weekend and will not return until Sunday evening. Holden leaves Ackley's room and decides on the spur of the moment to leave Pencey Prep immediately, rather than wait until Wednesday. He does not want to get home before his parents receive the letter of expulsion from the headmaster because his mother will be very upset. As he packs, he feels sad at the thought of leaving Pencey Prep. On his way out of the dorm, he pauses at the end of the corridor and "was sort of crying." But then he "yelled at the top of [his] goddam voice, 'Sleep tight, ya morons!'" in a feeble attempt to hide the sadness which he feels.

Analysis

Paradoxically, once again, Holden seeks out Ackley, the so-called "friend" of whom he is most critical, the person who gets on his nerves most of all. He has been vicious in describing Ackley's repulsive personal habits and selfish ways, yet when he needs comfort from someone, when he is hurting both physically and emotionally, he is drawn to Ackley. Why does he do this? He surely knows that Ackley is the least empathetic person he knows. Is he setting himself up for disappointment by expecting Ackley to be something he cannot be?

Salinger may be taking a second swipe at organized religion in this passage. In an earlier chapter, Ossenburger was portrayed as a devout Christian who, in the end, seemed to use religion to get

ahead. Here we have Ackley, unwilling to listen to Holden because he needs to get his sleep so he can go to Mass early the next morning. Moreover, with the question about joining a monastery, Ackley is angered when he thinks Holden is being critical of his religion. Yet his religious fervor does not translate into action. Ackley reminds one of the priest and Levite in the Good Samaritan Parable in the Gospel of Luke. The priest and Levite were religious, indeed, but make no effort to help a brother in need. In the name of religion, Ackley cannot stay awake to listen to a friend who is hurting.

Stradlater is equally unconcerned about Holden's welfare. There is blood all over Holden's face, but when Stradlater returns to the room, he makes no effort to check on Holden's condition. But this is very much in character for Stradlater.

In Chapter Six, Holden is critical of the athletes using Ed Banky's car even though it is against the rules. Yet, it is clear in this chapter that Holden was in Banky's car when he double-dated with Stradlater on a previous occasion. Is this another example of the phoniness Holden sees in everyone except himself?

Earlier, Holden expressed concern about not feeling anything about leaving Pencey Prep. Then in Chapter Five he refers to some pleasant memories (snowball fight in the beautiful snow after dinner, and a mention of Mal Brossard as his friend). Now he is feeling unmitigated sadness. He feels hurt and abandoned by his two friends. He feels guilty about hurting his mother. He feels all alone as he walks out of the dorm, and then almost falls down the steps because someone has thoughtlessly littered the stairwell with peanut shells.

Study Questions

1. Why does Ackley not want to play canasta?

2. Why does Holden become angry with Ackley?

3. When Ackley insists on hearing the reasons for the fight, how does Holden answer him?

4. What does Holden think about as he lies in Ely's bed?

5. What is it about Stradlater that makes him so dangerous on a date?

6. What makes Holden so lonely that he wakes up Ackley?
7. What is it that really upsets Ackley?
8. What does Holden decide when he leaves Ackley's room?
9. Why does packing his ice skates make Holden sad?
10. How does Holden feel as he is about to leave Pencey Prep?

Answers

1. Ackley says that it is late, and he has to get up early to go to Mass.

2. Holden is angry because Ackley is interested only in the reasons for the fight rather than providing comfort for Holden.

3. Holden says that the fight was over Stradlater's saying that Ackley had a lousy personality. Sadly, Ackley believes him, but then Holden tells him that he was kidding.

4. Holden does not think about his own pain and humiliation. Rather, he thinks about Jane and whether she was able to resist the allures of Stradlater.

5. Holden says that Stradlater has a sincere voice coupled with a handsome body, which make him irresistible to girls.

6. Holden is lonely because Stradlater returns to the room without showing any interest in Holden's well-being.

7. Holden asks Ackley about joining a monastery. Ackley interprets this as making fun of his religion.

8. Holden decides to leave Pencey Prep right away instead of waiting until Wednesday.

9. Holden reflects that his mother bought him this thoughtful gift, and he is disappointing her again by being expelled. He adds that almost every time someone gives him a present, it ends up making him sad.

10. Holden feels sad, but covers up his feelings by shouting, "Sleep tight, ya morons!"

Suggested Essay Topics

1. From Ackley's behavior in this chapter and from the description of Ossenburger in a previous chapter, how would you characterize Salinger's attitude toward organized religion?

2. What is Holden's attitude toward women based on the way he feels about Jane Gallagher?

3. In your judgment, how does Holden really feel about leaving Pencey Prep?

Chapter 8

New Characters:

Mrs. Morrow: *mother of Ernest Morrow, a classmate; the lady whom Holden met on the train*

Ernest Morrow: *a classmate of Holden's, son of the lady whom he met on the train*

Rudolf Schmidt: *the name of the janitor at Holden's dorm and the alias Holden used with Mrs. Morrow on the train*

Harry Fencer: *the president of Holden's class at Pencey Prep*

Summary

When Holden boards a train for New York, he meets the mother of one of his classmates at Pencey Prep, Mrs. Morrow. Because he finds Mrs. Morrow an attractive person, Holden makes up a story about her son, Ernest. Even though Ernest is not very likable, he tells her that Ernest is popular, but shy. In fact, he says, Ernest could have been president of the class, except that he would not allow his classmates to nominate him, out of shyness and modesty. By the time Holden finishes his story, Mrs. Morrow is extremely proud of her son. When Mrs. Morrow asks Holden if he is going home early because someone in his family is sick, he says that he is going home because he needs an operation. She is so sympathetic that Holden begins to feel guilty for the lies he has told.

Analysis

Once again, Holden, who is so quick to point out the phoniness in others, can, with equal speed, make up his own phony story. Authenticity is required of everyone except Holden. How is it that he can be so unforgiving when dealing with the perceived phoniness of others, yet so easily present himself as someone other than he really is? Given the chance to share himself with another person, a person whom he really likes (Mrs. Morrow), he decides to *create* a self to share. He does not have the courage to tell her who he really is. He uses a phony name. He does not have the courage to say that he was asked to leave Pencey because of his attitude toward formal education. In a word, he lacks the courage of his convictions. Holden struggles with authenticity and often does not measure up—much like the rest of us.

Holden's lies also take away from his credibility as a narrator. When we hear Holden lying for mere fun, we begin to wonder how much of what he is telling *us* is true. We might develop a skeptical attitude toward some aspects of the story since we now know that he can exaggerate and even invent elaborate stories off the top of his head.

Holden's description to the reader of Ernest is characteristically negative. But when Mrs. Morrow asks him about her son, he does not simply say something polite and nice. He creates a whole new persona for Ernest, a persona which fits what his mother would like him to be. She is, of course, very flattered. Holden tries to impress Mrs. Morrow with his maturity, albeit awkwardly, in his effort to reach out and make contact with another human being.

Study Questions

1. Why does Holden walk to the train station?
2. What does Holden say when asked whether he likes Pencey Prep?
3. Why is Mrs. Morrow concerned about Ernest?
4. Because Holden likes Mrs. Morrow, what does he tell her about Ernest?
5. According to Holden, why was Ernest Morrow not elected president of the class?

6. What does Mrs. Morrow suspect is the reason for Holden's going home late on a Saturday night?

7. What is Holden's explanation for going home on Saturday?

8. Why does Mrs. Morrow keep calling Holden by the name Rudolf?

9. Where does Mrs. Morrow invite Holden to visit Ernest in the summer?

10. What excuse does Holden give to Mrs. Morrow for not being able to visit Ernest in the summer?

Answers

1. Holden walks to the train station because it is too late to call a cab.

2. Holden tells Mrs. Morrow that it is as good as most schools, and that some of the faculty are "pretty conscientious."

3. Mrs. Morrow feels that Ernest is too sensitive and serious, and, thus, not a "terribly good mixer."

4. Holden tells Mrs. Morrow that Ernest is shy, modest, and one of the most popular boys at Pencey Prep.

5. Holden said that Ernest was not elected president because he would not allow his classmates to nominate him.

6. Mrs. Morrow suspects that someone in Holden's family may be sick.

7. Holden says that he needs an operation because he has a small brain tumor.

8. Holden told Mrs. Morrow that his name was Rudolf Schmidt.

9. Mrs. Morrow invites Holden to visit Ernest at Gloucester, Massachusetts during the summer.

10. Holden tells her that he will be going to South America with his grandmother in the summer.

Suggested Essay Topics

1. Why does Holden not give his real name when talking with Mrs. Morrow?

2. When he is with Mrs. Morrow, why does Holden pretend to be the "sophisticated man-about-town"?

3. What effect does it have on our reading when Holden tells us he can "go on lying for hours" if he "feels like it"?

Chapter 9

New Characters:

Phoebe: *Holden's younger sister*

Sally Hayes: *a close friend of Holden's*

Mrs. Hayes: *Sally's mother*

Carl Luce: *an acquaintance of Holden's from the Whooton School*

Faith Cavendish: *a former stripper, who would not meet Holden for a drink*

Eddie (Edmund) Birdsell: *a student at Princeton who gave Faith Cavendish's name and telephone number to Holden*

Anne Louise Sherman: *a girl whom Holden once dated*

Summary

When the train arrives at Penn Station, Holden goes into a phone booth and considers calling his brother, his sister, Jane Gallagher's mother, Sally Hayes, and Carl Luce. In the end, he decides to call no one. He then takes a cab to the Edmont Hotel—a budget hotel. His room is modest at best, and he can see from his room what is going on in rooms on the other side of the hotel. He describes what he sees as perversions. He is reminded of Stradlater, and how much he would have enjoyed the views from his window. In fact, Holden feels that Stradlater would have fit right in. Holden finally calls Faith Cavendish and asks her to join him for a cocktail. She is offended that a stranger would call her in the middle of the night. After they talk about their "mutual friend," she begins to

mellow and offers to meet him the following day. Holden, however, says he is too busy and later regrets this decision.

Analysis

This is the second time that Holden refers to the ducks in Central Park. The first time (Chapter Two) was during his discussion with Mr. Spencer about Holden's academic failure. Holden wonders what will become of the ducks. When the pond freezes, the ducks lose the place where they belong and the security of their home. Who will feed them? How will they survive? He appears to identify with the ducks. His feeling of alienation is illustrated in his reluctance to call family and friends. On two occasions, he has been unwilling to reach out to Jane Gallagher, using the excuse that he is not in the mood. Although this is not an adequate explanation, it does reveal the depth of his loneliness and depression. He chooses to contact a stranger rather than reach out to someone close to him. The spiritual and emotional nourishment that comes from family and friends is missing from his life. Who will feed Holden? Will he survive spiritually?

But why does he feel depressed and alienated? Consider for a moment his attitude toward almost everyone. Nobody meets his standards. Every person he looks at appears soiled, tainted, or odd, just like the people he sees from his hotel window. Biblical authors called it original sin. Holden will not accept that all human beings are tainted. Relationships, then, are possible only with flawed human beings. He says, referring to the people in the hotel, "I was probably the only normal bastard in the whole place...." What Holden does not realize is that he too is tainted, flawed, imperfect.

Yet Holden still expresses genuine empathy and caring for some people. Consider his description of the bellman. He expresses compassion for the man who, in his old age, must earn a living by carrying bags for others and then stand there and wait for a tip. Consider further his attitude toward women. In contrast to a character such as Stradlater, Holden feels that lovemaking should be done only with those whom one cares about. This is in sharp contrast to the Playboy philosophy which was beginning to emerge in the fifties, where it was implied that women are for the amusement of men. Sex does not require commitment. While Holden does have a sense of seriousness about sex, he claims "it is something I don't understand too hot . . . I keep making up these sex rules for myself, and then break them right away." While he understands the importance of setting certain principles for himself, he admits that he is not always able to live up to them.

Study Questions

1. What does Holden do when he reaches Penn Station?
2. What does Holden discuss with the cab driver on the way to the Edmont Hotel?
3. What is Holden's opinion of the Edmont Hotel?
4. How does Holden describe the bellman at the Edmont Hotel?
5. How does Holden feel about "necking" with girls whom he does not really care about?
6. What type of rules does Holden have difficulty observing?
7. What excuse has Holden planned to use in order to get through to Jane Gallagher on the telephone after-hours?
8. Why does Holden not call Jane Gallagher?
9. From whom did Holden get Faith Cavendish's name?
10. How does Holden feel after Faith Cavendish refuses to meet him for a cocktail?

Answers

1. Holden goes to a phone booth and considers calling D.B., Phoebe, Jane Gallagher's mother, Sally Hayes, and Carl Luce. He comes up with reasons for not calling any of them. In the end, he calls no one.
2. Holden asks the cab driver whether he knows what happens to the ducks in the Central Park lagoon when the pond freezes over.
3. Holden thinks the Edmont Hotel is "lousy with perverts." He thinks Stradlater would have fit right in.

4. Holden says the bellman looks to be about 65. He is even more depressing than the room—having to carry people's suitcases and wait around for a tip.

5. Holden feels that he should not "neck" or have sex with a girl unless he really cares about her. He, however, does admit to having trouble living up to his principles.

6. Holden makes up "these sex rules" for himself. He says that he then breaks them right away. Sex is something, he says, he just does not understand.

7. Holden is going to say that he is Jane's uncle and that her aunt has just been killed in a car accident.

8. Holden does not call Jane Gallagher because he says he is not in the mood (an excuse he has used before).

9. Holden obtained Faith's name and telephone number from Eddie Birdsell, a student at Princeton, whom Holden met at a party.

10. Holden regrets that he did not make a date to see Faith the next day.

Suggested Essay Topics

1. Why do you think Holden is concerned about the welfare of the ducks at Central Park during the winter?

2. Holden uses the excuse of not being in the mood for not calling Jane, just as he did in Chapter Four when he did not go to say hello to her. What do you suppose is the real reason that he does not want to make contact with her?

Chapter 10

New Characters:

Bernice: *one of the girls whom Holden met in the Lavender Room; blonde and a good dancer*

Marty: *one of the girls whom Holden met in the Lavender Room; a poor dancer*

Laverne: *one of the girls whom Holden met in the Lavender Room*

Summary

Holden spends a considerable amount of time talking to the reader about Phoebe, but dismisses the idea of calling her on the telephone. Instead, he goes downstairs to the Lavender Room, a lounge in the hotel. He is seated next to a table of three girls from Seattle, who are visiting New York City. He dances with them and tries to strike up a conversation, but they show little interest in him. They are interested only in spotting celebrities in the night club. Finally they decide to go to bed because they are going to the first show at Radio City Music Hall the next day. Holden is left to pay the bill.

Analysis

Holden contrasts his ten-year-old sister Phoebe's depth, maturity, and intelligence with the shallowness of three ordinary girls from Seattle. Phoebe sounds like a candidate for sainthood, as did Allie, when Holden described him in an earlier chapter. The innocence of children has a strong attraction for Holden. The adult world is still repulsive to him, counterfeit, and full of pretense. The band was "putrid," there were "whory-looking blondes" and "pimply-looking guys." Most of the people in the lounge were "old, show-offy-looking guys with their dates." Holden is critical of the girls for being superficial—constantly on the lookout for celebrities and attending an early daytime show at Radio City Music Hall, which he regards as touristic. Yet he is trying to impress them, much as he tried to impress Mrs. Morrow on the train. On one level, he is critical of the people in the hotel and lounge, yet, on another, he is indistinguishable from them. Holden is conventional while he casts stones at conventionality. He is smoking cigarettes, trying to order

alcoholic beverages, and trying to appear "cool," sophisticated, and worldly. But Holden is deeply disturbed as he finds himself simultaneously seduced and repulsed by the hollow values of the adult world.

Study Questions

1. Why does Holden decide not to call Phoebe?
2. How does Holden feel about Phoebe?
3. How much does Holden think it will cost him to get a prime table in the Lavender Room?
4. How does Holden know that the three girls at the next table are not from New York City?
5. How do the girls react when Holden asks them whether anyone wants to dance?
6. What does Bernice say that betrays how shallow she is?
7. Does Bernice enjoy dancing with Holden?
8. How does Holden overstep the bounds of propriety with Bernice?
9. Do the girls invite Holden to sit down at their table?
10. How does Holden describe the experience of dancing with Marty?

Answers

1. Holden is concerned that one of his parents will answer the telephone. Moreover, even if he hangs up, he thinks that his mother will know it is he because she is "psychic."
2. Holden is very fond of Phoebe. He says that she is pretty and smart. In a discussion, she understands exactly what you are talking about. She can distinguish a good movie from a bad one. She, however, is sometimes too affectionate and very emotional.
3. Holden thinks a dollar tip to the headwaiter will get him a good table.

4. Holden notices that their hats are not the kind commonly worn in New York City.

5. They giggle.

6. Holden is appalled by the fact that Bernice thinks seeing Peter Lorre in person the night before is significant.

7. No. She does not listen to Holden, and continues to look around, hoping to see a celebrity.

8. Holden kisses Bernice on the head, then uses profanity.

9. No. He sits down with them uninvited.

10. Holden says that dancing with Marty is like dragging the Statue of Liberty around the floor.

Suggested Essay Topics

1. Why does Holden try to make contact with three obviously unsophisticated girls from out of town?

2. Why does Holden take the liberty of kissing Bernice on the head?

Chapter 11

New Characters:

Mrs. Caulfield: *Holden's mother*

Mrs. Cudahy: *Jane's mother*

Mr. Cudahy: *Jane's stepfather*

Summary

    Having paid the check, Holden leaves the Lavender Room and begins thinking about Jane Gallagher. He sits down in a chair in the lobby of the hotel and gets upset again, thinking about what might have happened between Jane Gallagher and Stradlater. He is relatively certain that nothing happened, but he still gets disturbed when he thinks about it. He begins to reminisce about how he met Jane. They were neighbors at their summer homes in Maine the summer before last. He spent a good deal of time with Jane that summer, playing tennis and golf. Although their relationship was not especially romantic, it was intimate. Although they shared much, Jane did not share with him the nature of her conflict with her mother's husband, which was obviously very upsetting to her. After this digression about Jane Gallagher, Holden decides to go to Ernie's, a nightclub in Greenwich Village.

Analysis

Holden and Jane Gallagher each seem to have had an unhappy childhood. In Maine, they were comfortable with each other, and enjoyed playing golf, tennis, and other games together. Holden said they shared much; he even showed her Allie's baseball mitt. But there were limits. For example, Jane did not share with him the problem with her step-father and Holden, in his present moment of crisis, did not reach out to her when she was right on campus that very evening. Although Jane seems to be Holden's best friend, he does not want her to know that he was kicked out of Pencey Prep. It is difficult to understand how in this mood of attempting to fend off loneliness, he reaches out to Ackley, the taxi driver, the girls in the lounge, but not to Jane. Perhaps Holden is not all that dissatisfied with the phoniness that accompanies superficial relationships. He refuses to engage in the one relationship where he could find authenticity and comfort and, instead, pursues relationships that are guaranteed to be empty and phony at best.

Study Questions

1. Does Holden think that Stradlater seduced Jane Gallagher?
2. What sports does Jane Gallagher enjoy playing?
3. How did Jane Gallagher and Holden get to be friends?
4. What kind of books did Jane Gallagher like to read?
5. Is Jane Gallagher pretty?
6. What was it that made Jane Gallagher cry when she and Holden were playing checkers?
7. How important was necking in Holden's relationship with Jane Gallagher?

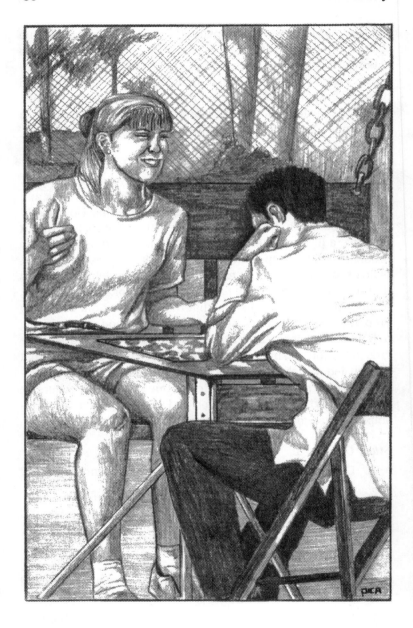

8. How does Holden know about Ernie's in Greenwich Village?
9. Who is Ernie?
10. What does Holden find especially irritating about Ernie?

Answers

1. No, he does not. But Holden says that it drives him crazy just thinking about it.
2. Jane Gallagher enjoys playing golf and tennis.
3. Jane Gallagher was a neighbor of Holden's at their summer houses in Maine. They met at the swimming pool at the club after an incident regarding her dog relieving itself on the Caulfield lawn.
4. Holden says that Jane reads very good books, including much poetry.
5. Holden's mother does not think Jane is pretty. But Holden says that he just liked the way she looked, that's all.
6. It had to do with her mother's husband. But Holden says that he never did find out what was the matter.
7. It was not important at all. Actually, they preferred to hold hands.
8. Ernie's is a night club in Greenwich Village which his brother, D.B., used to frequent.
9. Ernie is a fat, black man who plays the piano in the club.
10. Holden says that Ernie is a snob. He will talk to you only if you are a big shot or a celebrity.

Suggested Essay Topics

1. Use your creativity to describe the nature of the conflict between Jane Gallagher and her mother's husband.
2. Describe Holden's relationship with Jane Gallagher. Are they lovers? Just friends? More than just friends?

Chapter 12

New Characters:

Horwitz: *the cabdriver who takes Holden to Ernie's*

Ernie: *the owner of nightclub in Greenwich Village and featured piano player there*

Lillian Simmons: *a former girlfriend of D.B.'s, whom Holden meets in Ernie's*

Summary

Holden takes a cab to Ernie's, a night club in Greenwich Village. The cab driver, Horwitz, is impatient with Holden, and always sounds angry when he is talking. Holden asks him where the ducks go in the winter. Horwitz answers in an irascible manner that he does not know, but then begins talking about the fish in the lake. Although Holden is upset by his "touchy" manner, and decides that it is no pleasure discussing anything with him, he invites Horwitz to join him for a drink. Horwitz declines, and Holden enters Ernie's. Holden is irritated by Ernie because he thinks Ernie is a snob. He is irritated by the crowd which fawns over Ernie. He objects to the conversations which he overhears at two tables next to him. Lillian Simmons, a friend of his brother, D.B., says hello to him. He objects to her and her date. Depressed and lonely, he leaves Ernie's.

Analysis

Robert Burns has a line in his poem, "To a Louse," "Oh wad some power the giftie gie us/ To see oursels as others see us!" This should be Holden's motto. Consider this. He is appalled by the behavior of the Joe Yale-looking guy at the next table in Ernie's. The guy is talking to his date about the suicide attempt of a fellow student and, at the same time, groping her under the table. Yet in the previous chapter, Holden is guilty of the very same crudeness in his reaction to Jane Gallagher. Jane begins to cry when they are playing checkers. Holden tries to comfort her by sitting next to her and putting his arm around her. But he doesn't stop there. He begins kissing her—her eyes, her nose, her forehead, her eyebrows,

her ears, her whole face. Is he confusing lust with sympathy? Surely, he knows better than this. Is the Joe Yale-looking guy's behavior really any worse than Holden's?

The litany of references to loneliness and depression continues in this chapter. He refers to the loneliness of the streets. He seeks companionship from the cab driver, first by initiating conversation, and then asking that he join him for a drink. Even people applauding for Ernie depresses Holden because they applaud whether he plays well or poorly. He sees loneliness everywhere. Yet, when Holden is invited to sit with D.B.'s former girlfriend and her date, Holden, very much in character, can only interpret this as a phony invitation.

Right after Holden pays the cab fare, Horwitz gives him a little scolding. He reminds Holden that Mother Nature takes care of the fish, and chides him for not recognizing this. The reader cannot help wondering whether this is a parable for Holden, namely, that he should trust in Divine Providence (Mother Nature). If he did, perhaps, he would not be worried about the ducks (himself).

Study Questions

1. What is the main theme of the first paragraph?

2. How does Holden describe Horwitz's personality?

3. What does Holden discuss with Horwitz?

4. How does Holden characterize the patrons at Ernie's?

5. What is it that Holden objects to about the crowd at Ernie's?

6. Why does Holden feel sorry for Ernie?

7. Describe the conversations going on at tables next to Holden.

8. Who is Lillian Simmons?

9. From Lillian Simmons' point of view, what is most impressive about D.B.?

10. How does Holden feel about such social amenities as saying to someone, "Glad to have met you?"

Answers

1. The main theme of the first paragraph is loneliness. He mentions it twice as well as the ducks, symbols of loneliness and alienation.

2. Holden describes Horwitz as impatient and the type of man who always sounds angry about something when he speaks.

3. Holden discusses with Horwitz what happens to the ducks and fish in the Central Park lagoon in the winter.

4. Holden says that most of the patrons are college and prep school students who are jerks.

5. Holden objects to the fact that the crowd applauds Ernie whether he plays well or poorly.

6. Holden feels sorry for Ernie because Ernie may not know anymore whether he is playing well or poorly, since people applaud regardless of how he plays the piano.

7. At one table a guy was reviewing every play of a football game for his girlfriend. At another table a guy was discussing an attempted suicide at school while giving his girlfriend a feel under the table.

8. Lillian Simmons is a girl whom Holden's brother, D.B., used to date.

9. Lillian Simmons is most impressed by the fact that D.B. is a writer in Hollywood.

10. Holden dislikes using those expressions when he does not mean them. But he believes that "If you want to stay alive, you have to say that stuff...."

Suggested Essay Topics

1. Discuss Holden's loneliness and depression in terms of how it permeates the entire chapter.

2. Explain why Holden invites Horwitz for a drink after he observes how difficult it is to discuss anything with him.

Chapter 13

New Characters:

Raymond Goldfarb: *the boy with whom Holden got drunk on scotch in the chapel at the Wooton School*

Maurice: *the elevator operator who procured the prostitute for Holden*

Sunny: *the prostitute procured by Maurice*

Summary

Holden walks back to the hotel from Ernie's. On the way, he fantasizes about the student at Pencey Prep who stole his gloves. Holden admits that he would not have the courage to confront the thief without appearing weak. His lack of courage depresses him, and he decides to stop in a bar for a drink. For some unknown reason, he changes his mind and goes straight back to the hotel. The elevator operator at the hotel asks Holden if he would like some female companionship. Too embarrassed to decline but also because he was feeling so depressed, he says yes. When the girl comes to his room, he first asks her to stay and just talk with him, but then begs off with the excuse that he has just had surgery and is still recuperating. The girl demands more money from Holden than was agreed upon with the elevator operator. But Holden refuses to pay it. She leaves in a snit.

Analysis

The theme of this chapter is Holden's inability to act on his beliefs. He bemoans the fact that he would not be able to confront the person who stole his gloves and tell him exactly how he feels. His lack of inner strength prevents him from being able to speak his mind. He gets into a long, boring analysis of how "yellow" he is, precisely how lacking in fortitude he really is. His behavior at the hotel illustrates this character flaw. When Maurice, the elevator operator, offers him a girl for the evening, he does not have the courage to say no, despite his explanation earlier that sex should be in the context

of a relationship. He says he is still a virgin, but his long justification for this betrays his embarrassment. When Sunny, bored by all the talk, decides to get down to business, he makes up a story about why he is unable to have intercourse. The truth is that he does not want to. The one time he takes a stand is in his refusal to give Sunny the extra five dollars she requests for her services. Holden, like so many people, finds himself taking a stand on the insignificant, but not speaking up for the values he claims to espouse. As one might expect, Holden becomes even more depressed.

The interest that Holden shows Sunny at first reveals much about how lonely he is at this point. Even though he finds her "pretty spooky," he does not dismiss her as "phony," like he does everyone else. We might think, then, that when he asks her to stay and talk, this is not just a cop-out, but that he is pretty seriously depressed and seems to desire some companionship.

Study Questions

1. Why does Holden walk back to the hotel rather than take a cab?
2. What does Holden think about as he walks back to the hotel?
3. What kind of a drinker does Holden think he is?
4. How does Holden feel when he arrives back at the hotel?
5. What excuse does Holden give for agreeing to meet with the prostitute?
6. What does Holden think about a girl's ability to control herself in the heat of passion?
7. Does Holden look forward to meeting with the prostitute?
8. How does Holden feel when the prostitute takes off her dress?
9. When does Holden begin to feel sorry for Sunny?
10. What excuse does Holden give Sunny for not wanting to have sex with her?

Answers

1. Holden says that, sometimes, you get tired of riding in taxi cabs in the same way you get tired of riding in elevators. Suddenly, one has to walk, no matter how far or how high up.

2. Holden thinks about his stolen gloves and how he would not have the courage to confront the thief and hit him if provoked. He sees himself as cowardly.

3. Holden thinks he has the capacity to drink a great deal of alcohol without appearing to be drunk.

4. Although Holden is not sleepy, he is depressed. He says that he almost wishes he were dead.

5. Holden says that he was so depressed he did not even think.

6. Holden thinks that a girl cannot stop herself when she is in the heat of passion. So when a girl says to stop, he stops.

7. He vacillates between looking forward to meeting her and being nervous about the encounter.

8. Holden says that he feels more depressed than sexy.

9. Holden begins to feel sorry for Sunny when he hangs up her dress. He feels sad when he thinks of her buying the dress and the store employees not knowing that she is a prostitute.

10. Holden tells her that he has just had surgery and has not sufficiently recuperated.

Suggested Essay Topics

1. Why does Holden spend so much time discussing his cowardliness (the various degrees of being yellow)?

2. Discuss Holden's rationale for never having lost his virginity.

Chapter 14

New Characters:

Bobby Fallon: *a neighbor and friend of Holden in Maine several years ago*

Arthur Childs: *a student at the Whooton School with whom Holden discusses religious issues*

Summary

After Sunny leaves his room, Holden feels miserable and depressed. He begins reminiscing about Allie. When he finishes the story, he goes to bed. Holden feels like praying, but does not. He says that he cannot always pray when he feels like it. Instead, he reflects on discussions he has had with Arthur Childs about Jesus and the disciples. He again tries to pray but is obsessed by thoughts of Sunny calling him a crumb-bum. Suddenly there is a knock at the door. When he opens the door, he sees Sunny and Maurice, who have come to collect the additional five dollars. Maurice and Holden argue. Sunny takes the money from Holden's wallet and is ready to leave the room. Maurice continues to argue with Holden and punches him in the stomach on the way out. Holden, with the wind knocked out of him, fantasizes that he has been shot by Maurice. The fantasy ends like a movie, with Holden shooting his attacker and his girlfriend, Jane Gallagher, bandaging his wounds. The chapter concludes with Holden entertaining the notion of suicide. But it is clear that he is not serious.

Analysis

Holden says that when he is depressed, he thinks about Allie, and talks to him. Mostly he talks about the guilt he feels for not allowing Allie to go with him and a friend on their bikes to Lake Sedebego. In his conversation with Allie, Holden wants to lessen his guilt by changing the past. He keeps telling Allie to go home and get his bicycle and come along. But, of course, it is too late.

Although it is often foolish to read too much autobiography in a writer's work, Holden sounds like Salinger himself in that he says his parents belong to two different religions and the children are

atheists. It does not appear that Holden is really an atheist any more than Salinger is. Rather he simply has difficulty identifying with an institutional church which requires adherence to a body of formal beliefs. His beliefs in the boundless love of God are clear. He believes in mercy and forgiveness more than justice and retribution. He thinks that Judas is in heaven, in contrast to the belief of most Christians.

Holden also feels great empathy for Jesus because his friends were not any better than Holden's. The disciples were no more faithful to Jesus than Ackley or Stradlater were to Holden. Holden has difficulty accepting the fact that Jesus might have chosen flawed human beings for disciples. After all, Holden will have only perfect people as friends. Since children are perfect (uncorrupted by the world), Holden's only friends are children (Allie and Phoebe).

It could be argued that one cannot understand Holden without some knowledge of the Bible. Holden's reference to the lunatic in the tombs is a good example. The story is in Chapter Five of Mark's Gospel. The man, possessed by demons and living in the tombs, is described by Mark as having an "unclean spirit." Jesus often breathed on the person out of whom he was driving an evil spirit. He gave them a clean spirit. Holden makes many references to his breath and his shortness of breath, e.g., when Maurice punches him in the stomach. He is concerned about his breath being bad and makes references to others' bad breath. He himself feels that his breath is bad because of cigarettes and alcohol (symbols of corruption). Like the lunatic, Holden is mad and possessed by his own demons. He makes frequent use of the word "madman." It is on his mind constantly. He is mad because he is alone and possessed by the demons of alienation, death, meaninglessness, guilt, and despair. He inflicts pain on himself, like the lunatic, by putting himself in situations which are guaranteed to cause pain. His uncontrolled speech gets him hurt by both Stradlater and Maurice. He tries to make contact with people who disappoint him, e.g., Ackley, Stradlater, Faith Cavendish. Finally, he talks of suicide as a way of casting out these unclean spirits. Some would say that this entire book is about Holden's efforts to cast out his own demons before they destroy him.

Study Questions

1. After Sunny leaves Holden's room, whom does he begin talking to?

2. What is it that Holden finds disturbing about Jesus' disciples?

3. How does Holden's belief about Judas differ from that of his friend Arthur Childs?

4. How does Holden say that Jesus chose his disciples?

5. How does Holden know who is knocking on his door even before opening it?

6. Why do Maurice and Sunny return to Holden's room?

7. What is it about ministers that Holden does not like?

8. How does Maurice respond when Holden says that he is going to scream his head off if Maurice roughs him up?

9. What religion are the children in Holden's family?

10. What excuse does Holden give for not committing suicide by jumping out the window?

Answers

1. Holden begins talking to his dead brother, Allie.

2. Holden is disturbed that, although Jesus' disciples were all right after He died, they kept letting Him down while He was alive.

3. Holden believes that Jesus did not send Judas to Hell for betraying Him and committing suicide. Arthur Childs believes that Judas was sent to Hell.

4. Holden says that Jesus chose his disciples at random.

5. Holden says he knows who is knocking at the door because he is psychic.

6. Maurice and Sunny came to collect an additional five dollars for Sunny's services.

7. Holden does not like their phony "Holy Joe" voices.

8. Maurice implies that he will notify Holden's parents that he has been with a prostitute.

9. The children in Holden's family are all atheists.

10. Holden says that he does not "want a bunch of stupid rubbernecks looking at me when I was all gory."

Suggested Essay Topics

1. Discuss the significance of the fantasy about being shot which Holden conjures up after he is punched by Maurice.

2. After Holden has been willing to compromise on so many of his principles, why do you think Holden is willing to get beat up over five dollars?

Chapter 15

New Characters:

The Nuns: *two nuns whom Holden meets in Grand Central Station*

Dick Slagle: *Holden's roommate at Elkton Hills School*

Louis Shaney: *a Catholic boy at Whooton School whom Holden met in the infirmary*

Summary

Holden awakens at about 10:00 a.m. on Sunday. He considers having breakfast sent up to his room, but he is afraid that Maurice may be the one to bring it. Instead, he thinks about calling Jane Gallagher, decides against it, and then calls Sally Hayes. He arranges to meet Sally for an afternoon show. Concerned about his luggage, he decides to rent a locker at Grand Central Station. Once there, he has breakfast at the counter in the restaurant. While he is eating, two nuns come along and sit down next to him. Holden engages them in conversation. Both are teachers, one of English and one of history and American government. They discuss literature and all seem to enjoy the discussion. Holden, however, is a little uneasy because he thinks the nuns may try to find out whether he is Catholic. As the nuns leave, Holden is greatly embarrassed because he accidentally blows cigarette smoke in their faces. Once they are gone, he regrets not giving them more money.

Analysis

Holden continues his self-imposed alienation in this chapter. He thinks about calling Jane Gallagher and dismisses the idea. Of course, he is still not "in the mood." If anybody can make Holden feel better it is Jane. Instead, he calls Sally, sets up a date with her, and then notes that he finds her annoying. While having breakfast, he initiates a conversation with two nuns. At least on the subconscious level, he knows that he cannot have any kind of a long-lasting relationship with Sally or the nuns. He works hard at initiating temporary relationships. If he feels lonely, it is his own doing. It is clear by now that he reaches out only to people who cannot or will not help him.

The nuns are in the world but not of the world. Thus, Holden is attracted to them. They are like Phoebe and Jane, innocent and untarnished by the world. They need to be looked after so he gives them a donation. They are so much not of the world that he is even embarrassed talking to them about Romeo and Juliet, since there is sex in the play.

Holden is absolutely mortified when he accidentally blows smoke in the faces of the nuns. This is sacrilegious because his breath tainted by smoke is symbolic of his unclean spirit. Their spirits are clean and pure, and he defiles them.

How appropriate that Holden should go to Grand Central Station. It attracted him like a magnet. It symbolizes all that is impermanent in life. Grand Central Station is not a place you stay in but a place you pass through. All relationships there are, by nature, superficial and temporary. Despite what Holden says to the contrary, Holden seeks out the "temporary." Metaphorically, Grand Central Station is the perfect place for him.

Finally, Holden regrets not giving the nuns more money. But then his life has been a series of regrets.

Study Questions

1. When Holden awakens on Sunday morning, he thinks about the time of his last meal. When was that?

2. Whom does Holden think about calling when he awakens?

3. Where is Sally supposed to meet Holden?

4. Why does Holden not want to tell his mother that he was expelled again?

5. Why did Dick Slagle take Holden's suitcases out from under the bed and put them out where they could be seen?

6. What was Dick Slagle's favorite word?

7. Why did Holden miss Dick Slagle after they were given different roommates?

8. What subjects do the two nuns teach?

9. What does Holden find annoying about Catholics?

10. Holden says that he did something stupid and embarrassing when the two nuns got up to leave. What was it?

Answers

1. Holden's last meal was the two hamburgers he had with Brossard and Ackley, the night before.

2. Holden thinks about calling Jane Gallagher, but decides against it because he is not in the mood.

3. Sally is supposed to meet Holden under the clock at the Biltmore Hotel.

4. Holden does not want to tell his mother about the expulsion because her health has not been good since Allie died. Holden says that she is very nervous.

5. Dick Slagle wanted people to think that Holden's expensive luggage was his own.

6. Dick Slagle's favorite word was bourgeois.

7. Holden missed Dick Slagle because he had a good sense of humor and they sometimes had much fun together.

8. One teaches English and the other teaches history and American government.

9. Holden says that Catholics are always trying to find out whether you are Catholic or not.

10. Holden is embarrassed by the fact that he accidentally blew cigarette smoke in their faces.

Suggested Essay Topics

1. Why do you suppose that Holden prefers to meet Sally Hayes rather than Jane Gallagher?

2. How does Holden feel about associating with people who are not as wealthy as he is?

3. Why do you think Holden enjoys talking to the nuns?

Chapter 16

New Characters:

Miss Aigletinger: *a former teacher of Holden's who frequently took her class to the Museum of Naural History*

Gertrude Levine: *Holden's partner when the class went to the Museum of Natural History*

Summary

When Holden finishes breakfast, he goes for a long walk. He thinks about the nuns collecting money for the poor. It makes him sad that the nuns never go anywhere nice for lunch. He walks toward Broadway, looking for a record store where he can buy *Little Shirley Beans*, a hard-to-find recording he wants to give to Phoebe. He notices a poor family, on their way home from church, and is intrigued by the six-year-old boy, who is singing, "If a body catch a body coming through the rye." The song lifts Holden's spirits. He observes many people on their way to the movies and is puzzled by the popularity of movies. The first music store he comes upon has *Little Shirley Beans*. He is delighted with his purchase and eager to give his gift to Phoebe. Holden goes into a drugstore and calls Jane Gallagher. But when her mother answers, he hangs up. He is still "not in the mood." After looking in the theater section of the newspaper, he decides to buy two tickets for *I Know My Love*. Holden says that this will impress Sally, the "queen of the phonies." In order to kill time, Holden takes a cab to the park and watches the children play. He has a short conversation with a girl around Phoebe's age, whose mention of the museum where Holden used to go reminds him of his own youth. As he walks through the park to the Museum

of Natural History, he happily remembers his frequent visits to the
museum with his class. What he especially liked was that nothing
ever changed in the museum. Everything always remains the same.
The only thing that ever changes is you. He fully intends to go into
the museum, but when he gets there, he finds it impossible to go in.

Analysis

As Holden observes the poor family on his walk, his attention
is drawn to a little boy singing a song ("If a body catch a body coming through the rye"). Holden's interest in this is almost a
celebration of the innocence of childhood. The boy is the quintes-
sence of childhood innocence. He walks in the street, but close to
the curb. He sings a song oblivious to his parents and everything
around him, including the traffic. The mention of this song is a
hint of what is to come in the explanation of the title of the book.

Holden cannot seem to mask his disbelief, even irritation, at
seeing so many people going to the movies on a Sunday afternoon.
No doubt he objects to the artificiality of movies, i.e., they are a
poor imitation of life itself—another variation of phoniness. Nev-
ertheless, he himself is going to a play in the afternoon, which he
says is only slightly more respectable than movies. He says that
actors try to be real, but actually end up just sounding the way
actors sound and not like real people.

As he observes the children at play in Central Park, Holden
seems to have forgotten that he is depressed. He genuinely enjoys
watching the children and remembers the good times of his own
childhood. He remembers with pleasure the Museum of Natural
History because nothing changes inside. Year after year, the displays remain the same. The only changes that occur take place
within the people looking at the displays. He fully intends to go
inside the museum, but when he gets there, he suddenly finds himself unable to do so. It is as if his own childhood is drawing to a
close, and there is a foreshadowing of adulthood, wherein changes
are not only inevitable, but manageable.

Holden's enthusiasm for buying Phoebe a gift is a rare positive
moment for him, matched only perhaps, by his unsolicited donation of ten dollars to the two nuns earlier. Even though he is running
out of cash, he pays five dollars for the record. The gift is purely a

sign of affection for his sister. For once, there is no hint of cynicism. After making this great find, he can hardly wait to give it to her. This is Holden at his best.

Study Questions

1. What makes Holden sad when he thinks about the nuns?
2. How did the little boy walking with his family lift Holden's spirits?
3. What kind of shows does Sally Hayes like to see?
4. Although Holden is getting low on cash, he takes a cab to the park instead of the subway. Why?
5. What is it about Phoebe's liking to skate near the bandstand that Holden thinks is funny?
6. Why is the young girl in the park having trouble tightening her skate?
7. How does Holden feel while he thinks about Miss Aigletinger taking his class to the museum?
8. What is it about Gertrude Levine, his partner at the museum, that Holden remembers?
9. According to Holden, what is the best thing about the museum?
10. Is Holden looking forward to his date with Sally?

Answers

1. What makes Holden sad is that the nuns never get to go anywhere swanky for lunch.
2. The boy was singing, "If a body catch a body coming through the rye."
3. Sally likes shows which are sophisticated and dry.
4. Holden wants to get off Broadway as fast as he can.
5. The bandstand is the same place where Holden liked to skate when he was a child.

6. The little girl does not have any gloves on and her hands are red and cold.

7. These pleasant memories make Holden feel very good.

8. Gertrude always wanted to hold Holden's hand, but her hand was always sweaty.

9. Everything always stays the same; nothing changes.

10. No, he seems to regret having made the date.

Suggested Essay Topics

1. Why does Holden feel less depressed after he hears the child sing, "If a body catch a body coming through the rye?"

2. Holden says that he does not like any shows very much and that movies are worse. Aside from the fact that he does not like actors, why do you think Holden feels this way?

3. Discuss why you think Holden changes his mind about going into the museum.

Chapter 17

New Characters:

Harris Macklin: *a roommate of Holden's for a couple of months at Elkton Hills School*

George something: *an acquaintance of Sally Hayes whom she saw at the play*

Summary

Holden sits in the lobby at the Biltmore Hotel and does some girl-watching while he waits for Sally Hayes to arrive. He muses about what will become of these girls. On the one hand, he considers that many will marry boring guys who are not intelligent. Then he remembers an old roommate of his, Harris Macklin, who was intelligent and boring too. Holden concludes that it may not be so bad if the girls marry boring guys, just so long as they are nice. Finally, he sees Sally coming up the steps. They greet each

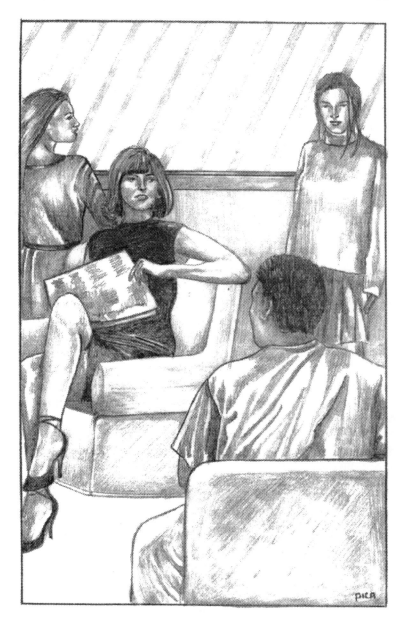

other and immediately take a cab to the theater. Naturally, Holden does not like the play. He dislikes the small-talk which he overhears during the intermissions. He especially was exasperated with the conversation between Sally and her friend, George. After the show, Sally suggests that they go ice skating at Radio City. Holden says that they are the worst skaters on the ice. He suggests that they stop skating and have a drink inside. Once they sit down, Holden quickly maneuvers the conversation to what he wants to talk about: that he is bored, depressed, and wants to move to Vermont and settle down with Sally. The absence of practical considerations from his plan frightens Sally. Holden says that he does not want to enter the "rat race" after college. Sally argues that he consider the practicality of his plan. Finally, Holden loses his temper and insults her. Sally is deeeply offended, and angered, and will accept no apology. Then Holden laughs at her. At this point, Sally insists that he leave. He does.

Analysis

In this chapter, Holden's story is beginning to heighten in intensity. Holden has never been a typical teenager, but now he is sounding desperate in his confusion. He regrets having made the date with Sally Hayes. Yet as soon as he sees her in the hotel, he thinks that he loves her and wants to marry her. He then admits that he does not even like her very much. When they are in the cab on the way to the play, Holden begins kissing Sally, but she is reluctant to respond. According to Holden, however, he is so seductive she cannot control herself. So much for Holden's speech about the necessity of having a relationship with a girl before he "makes out" with her. When they take a break from skating, he pours out to her the depression he feels about the meaninglessness of his life. His impulsive solution is that they run off together to Massachusetts and Vermont. Sally is the first person with whom he has shared these personal thoughts, yet he knows that she is incapable of understanding what he is talking about. Finding no empathy, he becomes angry and insults her. Holden really is beginning to sound like a "madman." It is as if he is a prisoner of the emotion of the moment. He uses the madman excuse more than ever for explaining why he is not acting on what he believes and saying what he means. Is this a classic pattern of self-destruction, or is he feeling internal pressure to come to terms with the passage to adulthood?

Study Questions

1. Why is Holden depressed when he is sitting in the lobby of the Biltmore?

2. Name two outstanding characteristics of Harris Macklin.

3. What is the best thing Holden can say about bores?

4. After Sally tells Holden that she loves him, how does she want to change him?

5. Holden says that the Lunts do not act like people or actors. What does he say they act like?

6. Why does Sally not talk much during the intermission?

7. What article of clothing does Holden associate with "Ivy League types?"

8. Why does Holden think that Sally really wants to go skating?

9. How do Holden and Sally's skating ability compare with the others who are on the ice?

10. Does Sally like school?

Answers

1. Holden says it is depressing when he keeps wondering about what will become of all the girls when they finish school.

2. He was very intelligent and was a good whistler.

3. They do not hurt anyone—most of them. In addition, they might have a special talent like being able to whistle well.

4. Sally wants Holden to let his hair grow.

5. Holden says that the Lunts act like they know they are celebrities, i.e., they are too good as actors.

6. Sally does not talk much, according to Holden, because she is busy looking around and being charming.

7.   Holden associates checkered vests with "Ivy League types."

8.   Holden thinks that Sally wants to go skating so she can wear one of those little skating skirts.

9.   Holden says that Sally and he are the worst skaters on the ice.

10. Sally says that school is a terrific bore.

Suggested Essay Topics

1.   Explain the following statement of Holden's: "...I told her I loved her and all. It was a lie, of course, but the thing is, I meant it when I said it." What does this have to do with Holden always calling himself a "madman"? In what ways might this and other contradictions be said to be acting "crazy"?

2.   Discuss why you think Holden would not tell his roommate that he was an excellent whistler.

3.   Discuss why Holden laughs at Sally while she is angry.

4.   Discuss what Holden means when he says that although he would not have taken her up to New England, if she had wanted to go, he meant it when he asked her to go with him.

Chapter 18

New Characters:

Al Pike: *Jane Gallagher's date at a Fourth of July dance*

Bob Robinson: *a friend of Holden's who had an inferiority complex*

Summary

Holden leaves the skating rink and goes to a drugstore to get something to eat. He considers calling Jane Gallagher to ask her to go dancing. Thinking of Jane reminds him of a story about Jane and her date, Al Pike, at a Fourth of July dance. Not surprisingly, Holden was critical of Al in front of Jane, labeling him as a show-off.

Jane excused Al's behavior by saying he was not a show-off, but had an inferiority complex. In an effort to explain to the reader the difference between someone with an inferiority complex and a show-off, Holden describes his friend Bob Robinson. He really did have an inferiority complex since he felt inferior because his parents were uneducated and not wealthy.

Holden calls Jane but there is no answer. He then calls Carl Luce, a fellow whom Holden remembers (but, of course, does not like) from Whooton, who is now attending Columbia University. They agree to meet at 10:00 p.m. at the Wicker Bar for drinks.

In order to pass the time until then, Holden goes to Radio City to see a movie. He is critical of the Christmas show as well as the movie. The Christmas show is a gaudy pseudo-religious spectacle. The movie is about an Englishman, who was wounded in the war and loses his memory. But in the end he regains his memory, gets the girl, and they all live happily ever after. After the movie, Holden begins walking to the Wicker Bar. On the way, he thinks about war and his brother D.B.'s experiences in the army. Holden concludes that he is opposed to war, but not necessarily from principle. He is opposed to war because, as a soldier, he would have to associate with undesirables, like Ackley, Stradlater, and Maurice.

Analysis

While most people would be quite upset by the quarrel he had with Sally, it does not seem to bother Holden. He does not even mention her in this chapter. Holden feels no remorse for hurting her. Yet he is critical of the insensitivity of the woman sitting next to him in the theater. Although she cries throughout the movie, she will not inconvenience herself to take her child to the restroom.

Even though he does not reach her, Holden is at least trying to call Jane Gallagher. Up to this point, he has not been "in the mood." But she is still out of reach. Thinking of Jane reminds him of a story about a boyfriend of hers, and he remarks that if a girl likes a guy, she will overlook all his faults. If she does not like him, she will see no good in him. What he fails to recognize is that most people do this, not just girls.

By calling Carl Luce, Holden once again calls someone who really cannot help him. He does not like Carl and never did. Carl's

presence brings out the worst in Holden. But Holden prefers the company of someone he does not like to being alone.

Holden is not meeting Carl Luce until later that evening, so he takes in the stage show and movie at Radio City. Curiously enough, he laughed at the girls from Seattle for going to Radio City. Of course, Holden sees the stage show as gaudy, showy, and cheap. His description of the movie sounds like a Harlequin Romance on-screen. He told us earlier why he does not like movies and actors. One cannot help asking, what else does he expect?

When he begins talking about war, Holden sets up the expectation that he will take the moral high ground and oppose war of any kind. But his only concern is that if he were in the army, he would have to associate with the likes of Ackley and Stradlater. Selfish preferences seem to hold the highest place in his value system.

Study Questions

1. After Holden leaves the skating rink, where does he go?

2. In Holden's opinion, how do girls defend a boy they like if someone criticizes him by calling him mean or conceited?

3. Why did Bob Robinson have an inferiority complex?

4. Why does Holden go to Radio City after he leaves the drugstore?

5. According to Holden, what is there about the show at Radio City that Jesus would really like?

6. In the movie, what happens to Alec that causes him to regain his memory?

7. Why is Holden so critical of the lady who sits next to him in the movie?

8. What kind of job did D.B. have when he was overseas in the army?

9. In Holden's opinion, what was inconsistent about D.B.'s liking the novel *A Farewell to Arms*?

10. Why is Holden happy that the atomic bomb has been invented?

Answers

1. Holden goes to the drugstore to get something to eat.

2. The girls say he has an inferiority complex.

3. Bob had an inferiority complex because his parents were uneducated and not wealthy.

4. Holden goes to Radio City to pass the time until he meets Carl Luce at ten o'clock that evening.

5. Holden says that Jesus would really like the guy in the orchestra who plays the kettle drums.

6. Alec gets hit in the head with a cricket ball.

7. Holden is critical of his seatmate because she cries throughout the movie as if she were kindhearted, but refuses to take her child to the restroom during the movie.

8. D.B. was the driver for a general.

9. Holden did not understand how D.B. could hate war and like the novel *A Farewell to Arms*.

10. Holden says if there is another war he would sit on top the bomb rather than go into the army.

Suggested Essay Topics

1. Discuss whether you think Holden's attitude toward war foreshadowed the anti-war movement of the sixties.

2. What does Holden mean when he says that he is glad that the atomic bomb has been invented?

3. Why do you think some people (like Holden) find religious tributes by the theater offensive, e.g., the Christmas show at Radio City Music Hall?

Chapter 19

Summary

Holden arrives at the Wicker Bar before Luce. While he is waiting, he describes the Wicker Bar as a sophisticated place which is frequented by phonies and homosexuals. Holden regards the bartender as a snob. Luce finally arrives and makes it clear that he cannot stay for very long. The conversation goes from bad to worse. Holden is able to irritate Luce with every statement he makes and every question he asks. Although Holden recognizes that many of his questions are too personal, he continues asking them and justifies his behavior to himself by arguing that Luce, as student advisor, used to ask questions that were too personal. Finally, Luce repeats the advice which he gave Holden the last time they were together: that Holden should consult a psychoanalyst. They continue to trade insults (Holden's are oblique; Luce's are direct). As Luce leaves, Holden, desperately lonely, practically begs him to stay and have another drink with him. Luce, however, declines because he is already late for a date.

Analysis

Although Holden can hardly wait to tell us how pseudo-sophisticated the Wicker Bar is, he includes the fact that he himself used to go there frequently. Needless to say, this contradictory behavior is in character for Holden. For example, he dislikes movies and plays, but goes to them frequently. He finds Ernie's night club in the Village disgusting, but he goes there. Now the Wicker Bar is not up to his standards, yet he chooses it as a place to meet Luce. Is Holden doing all the "right" things, e.g., ordering scotch, smoking cigarettes, going to night clubs, so that he can appear to be sophisticated and mature? Yet there is another part of him that knows these are empty values. How many young people are beguiled by the glamour of sophisticated behaviors as they make their way on the path to adulthood? How many adults are still beguiled by it?

Earlier in the book when Holden fought with Stradlater, he said that he was not too tough and had been in only about two fights in his life. While that may be true, he uses words instead of punches

and seeks out verbal fights. In the argument with Stradlater, Holden was hit physically because he continued to attack Stradlater verbally. Holden was punched by Maurice only because he kept insulting him. Now with Luce, Holden manages to alienate and offend him with every word that comes out of his mouth. Rather than striking Holden as did Stradlater and Maurice, Luce silences Holden by simply leaving. Holden's behavior is clearly self-destructive because, although he desperately wants companionship, his insufferable behavior prevents it. One wonders whether Luce would have stayed longer if Holden's behavior had been more civil.

Study Questions

1. Describe the entertainment at the Wicker Bar.
2. What types of people frequent the Wicker Bar?
3. Why does Holden not like the bartender at the Wicker Bar?
4. What was the relationship between Luce and Holden when they were at Whooton together?
5. What word does Luce use frequently?
6. How old is Luce's current girl friend?
7. Give one reason why Luce prefers Eastern philosophy to Western philosophy.
8. What is one of the annoying things about Luce, according to Holden?
9. What advice did Luce give to Holden?
10. What is the one positive thing Holden says about Luce at the end of the chapter?

Answers

1. Entertainment is provided by two French girls, Tina and Janine. Tina plays the piano and Janine sings.
2. According to Holden, the Wicker Bar is frequented by phonies and homosexuals.

3. Holden does not like the bartender because he considers him a snob. Holden says the bartender will hardly talk to you unless you are a big shot or a celebrity.

4. Luce was Holden's student advisor.

5. Holden says that Luce used to say "certainly" very often.

6. Luce is not certain, but he estimates that she is in her late thirties.

7. According to Luce, Eastern philosophies regard sex as both a physical and a spiritual experience.

8. Holden says that at Whooton, Luce would make you describe the most personal things that happened to you. But if you asked him personal questions, he became angry.

9. Luce advised Holden that he should consult a psychoanalyst.

10. Holden says that Luce has a good vocabulary; he had the largest of any boy at Whooton.

Suggested Essay Topics

1. Holden describes the Wicker Bar as sophisticated, but he is critical of the people who patronize it. Discuss why you think Holden chose the Wicker Bar as a place to meet Luce.

2. Discuss how you feel about Luce. Give reasons why you think he is or is not an appealing character.

Chapter 20

Summary

Luce escapes from the irascible Holden. Holden remains at the bar, watches the entertainment, and gets drunk. Because he is drunk and under age, he is careful not to draw attention to himself. He once again begins to fantasize about having a bullet in his stomach. Holden decides to call Jane Gallagher and leaves the bar. But as one might expect, he changes his mind because he is not "in the mood." Instead, he calls Sally Hayes and tells her that he will come to her house on Christmas Eve and help decorate the tree. Afterwards, though, he regrets having made the call. In an effort to become sober, he goes into a restroom and dunks his head in a sink of cold water. Still feeling depressed and lonely, he goes to the checkroom and gets his coat and the record he purchased for Phoebe. Holden walks to Central Park to see what has happened to the ducks. As he arrives at the park, he drops Phoebe's record and it breaks on the ground. Clearly upset, he picks up the pieces of the record, puts them in his pocket, and walks into the park. He finds the lagoon, but there are no ducks. As Holden sits shivering on a bench, he worries that he will come down with pneumonia and die. This leads him to thinking about his funeral and that of his brother, Allie. Holden feels sorry for his mother and father, particularly his mother since she is still grieving for Allie. The whole notion of being buried with dead people and visitors coming to the cemetery is troubling to him. Holden becomes obsessed thinking about how devastated Phoebe would be if he died. The thought of her grieving drives him to go see her at once, in effect, to finally go home.

Analysis

The tension and anxiety within Holden are building to a climax in this chapter. He reacts negatively to absolutely everyone and every situation. Valencia does not sing well. The headwaiter probably will not deliver his message (people never give your message to anybody). He calls Sally, then regrets having called her. Holden looks at himself and sees a wounded man (the bullet in his gut). He is not proud of the course his life has taken up to this point. It is as if life is draining out of him. He remarks that he has no place to go and does not know where he will sleep. Holden sees his lot as identical to the ducks he cannot find, and who are also homeless. The broken record symbolizes an end to this period in his life. His youth, his past, is irrevocably gone. But the thought of changing his life is terrifying. Change reminds him of Allie's death; it reminds him of his own death. He sees death as the quintessential change.

The critical moment has arrived. From the beginning, Holden has avoided going home. He now makes the decision. He decides to go home because he wants to see Phoebe in case he dies. But seeing Phoebe is just a subterfuge, a means to the end, i.e., going home is a dramatic realization that he must confront his past *as well as* his future. Going home is about accepting himself, including his strengths as well as his limitations and mistakes. Going home is about facing reality.

Study Questions

1. After Valencia sings, what does Holden ask the headwaiter to do?

2. When Holden leaves the Wicker Bar, why is he holding his stomach?

3. After Holden talks to Sally Hayes on the telephone, how does he picture her at home that evening?

4. While in the restroom, what advice does Holden give the piano player at the Wicker Bar?

5. What excuse does the lady in the hat-check room give Holden for not going on a date with him?

6. Because it is dark and spooky, what does Holden say he would do if he happened to see someone in Central Park?

7. What does Holden say he wants done with his body when he dies?

8. Why was Holden not able to attend his brother, Allie's, funeral?

9. While at the lagoon in Central Park, Holden counts his money. What does he do with the coins?

10. What is it that Holden worries about after he decides to go home and see Phoebe?

Answers

1. Holden asks the headwaiter to ask Valencia to join him for a drink.

2. Holden is holding his stomach because he is fantasizing that he is bleeding from a gunshot wound.

3. Holden pictures Sally at home with her date from Andover and the Lunts, all having tea, and having a sophisticated and phony conversation.

4. Holden advises the piano player that he needs a manager.

5. The lady in the hat-check room tells Holden that she is old enough to be his mother.

6. Holden says he probably would jump about a mile.

7. Holden says that he wants to be dumped in the river—anything rather than being buried in a cemetery.

8. Holden did not attend his brother's funeral because he was in the hospital as a result of injuries sustained when he learned of his brother's death.

9. Holden skips the quarters and the nickel across the pond.

10. Holden is concerned that he will waken his parents and they will catch him sneaking into the house.

Suggested Essay Topics

1. Discuss the significance of the increased frequency of Holden's references to his loneliness and depression.

2. Discuss Holden's preoccupation with dying in this chapter.

Chapter 21

Summary

Holden enters the family apartment, unrecognized, because there is a substitute elevator boy, whom he deceives. He sneaks into the apartment and finds Phoebe, not in her own room, but asleep in D.B.'s room. Holden says he feels good being home. He wakes up Phoebe, and both are obviously happy to see each other. Phoebe immediately asks him if he received her letter, in which she invited him to attend her play. He assures her that he is, indeed, coming to her play. They talk about where their parents have gone for the evening, the movie Phoebe saw that afternoon, the broken record, whether D.B. is coming home for Christmas, and that she had hurt her arm. But when Phoebe gets Holden to admit that he has been kicked out of school again, she explodes with anger and rejects him. Completely exasperated, she puts her head under a pillow and refuses to talk to him.

Analysis

Phoebe clearly brings out the best in Holden. He says that he actually feels good for a change. He is glad to be home and is resigned to the fact that if his parents find him, he will just have to accept it. In fact, it almost appears that he wants to be caught, given the fact that he is smoking and willing to take a chance on waking up his mother who is a light sleeper. Before Holden wakes Phoebe, he goes about the room looking at her clothes and things with affection and pride. As he reflects on these accouterments of childhood, he seems to be preparing himself for the ordeal of putting his youth behind him, and foreshadowing the quasi-religious calling he sees for himself in the next chapter.

Study Questions

1. When Holden gets on the elevator, whom does he tell the operator he is going to visit?

2. Holden is very skillful at opening the door quietly. What profession does he say he should have gone into?

3. When Holden enters the family apartment, how does he know for sure that he is in the right apartment?

4. How does Holden describe his mother's hearing ability?

5. Why does Phoebe not like her own room?

6. During the first few moments that he is in Phoebe's room, Holden says something he has not said for many chapters. What is it?

7. Holden's mother has outstanding tastes in what area?

8. What kind of reading does Holden find very interesting?

9. How did Phoebe hurt her arm?

10. What does Holden say that he may do now that he has been expelled from school?

Answers

1. Holden tells the elevator operator that he is going to visit the Dickstein Family.

2. Holden is so skillful at opening the door quietly, he says that he should have been a crook.

3. Holden knows that he is in the right apartment because their apartment has a distinctive smell.

4. Holden says that his mother can hear like a bloodhound (sic!).

5. Phoebe does not like her own room because it is too small.

6. Holden says the he feels "swell" for a change. He just feels good.

7. Holden's mother has outstanding taste in buying clothes.

8. Holden enjoys reading a child's school notebook.

9. Phoebe hurt her arm when Curtis Weintraub, a classmate, pushed her down the stairs in the park.

10. Holden says that he may get a job on a ranch in Colorado.

Suggested Essay Topics

1. Explain why you think Holden enjoys reading a child's school notebook.

2. Explain what Holden may mean when he describes his sister as "quite affectionate" for a child.

Chapter 22

New Character:

James Castle: *the boy who committed suicide at Elkton Hills School*

Summary

After leaving Phoebe to get cigarettes in the living room, Holden returns to the bedroom. Phoebe's response to Holden's expulsion is "Daddy'll kill you." Holden says that his dad will either send him to a military school, or that nothing will happen because Holden will be on a ranch in Colorado. Phoebe continues to press Holden as to why he was expelled. He resents the questioning and says that he is tired of everyone asking him that question. Holden, however, does tell Phoebe how bad it was at Pencey. He mentions all the phonies and mean guys there. Holden sums up his feelings when he exclaims, "I can't explain. I just didn't like anything that was happening at Pencey. I can't explain." Equally exasperated, Phoebe sternly says to Holden that he does not like anything. Phoebe challenges him to name one thing that he likes a lot. The challenge takes him by surprise, and the only things that come to mind are the nuns he met in the restaurant and James Castle, a boy at Elkton Hills who committed suicide. Finally, he responds that he likes Allie and likes being with Phoebe. Phoebe asks Holden to think of what he would like to be. She suggests that he might become a scientist or a lawyer. But he rejects them both. Holden then announces to Phoebe that he would like to be "the catcher in the rye," the protector, who watches over the children, and keeps them from falling off a cliff at the edge of a field of rye.

Analysis

Phoebe speaks for all of us when she confronts Holden with, "You don't like *anything* that's happening." Holden finds fault with everyone and everything to the exasperation of Phoebe and the reader. She finally says what most readers probably have been wanting to say to him throughout the book. Holden is caught off guard by her directness and is clearly embarrassed as he tries to respond. His first thought is of the nuns and James Castle. He is greatly impressed by the nuns' altruism and dedication. He is equally moved by the convictions, however misplaced, of James Castle.

It is fascinating that Holden has such admiration for the nuns' altruism, considering that up to this point he has demonstrated very little of it himself. He also admires James Castle for taking a stand for what he believes (warped though it is). Although Holden talks a "good game" about his convictions, the only times he stood up for anything was when he insisted on calling Stradlater a moron (and got beat up) and when he vociferously objected to the five dollar surcharge exacted by Maurice (when Holden got beat up again). One cannot help observing that the things Holden is willing to stand up for are almost as trivial as what James Castle died for.

The altruism of the nuns leads Holden to the concept of altruism in general. Holden wonders how one can be sure that his/her motives are pure: Am I doing good because I care about the welfare of others, or am I doing good for praise and recogniton? Because he cannot be sure of his motivation, Holden has an excuse to do nothing. The notion of the catcher in the rye is noble, but what does Holden mean? How will he translate this into real life? Holden gives flesh and blood to the cliche: talk is cheap.

Study Questions

1. To what does Holden compare Phoebe's behavior when she finds out that he was expelled from Pencey?

2. Where does Holden say that his father will send him when he learns that Holden has been expelled?

3. Even though Holden likes Mr. Spencer, why does he consider him a phony?

4. What was the Pencey alumnus looking for when he came to Holden and Stradlater's dorm?

5. When Holden thinks about the nuns, what does he picture them doing?

6. Why did James Castle commit suicide?

7. What was the topic of the only conversation that Holden remembers having with James Castle?

8. What habit of Holden's does Phoebe wants him to change?

9. What bothers Holden about becoming a lawyer?

10. Who is the author of "if a body meet a body coming through the rye?"

Answers

1. Holden compares Phoebe's behavior to that of the fencing team at Pencey who ostracized him after he left the foils on the subway.

2. Holden says that his father will send him to a military school.

3. Holden considers Mr. Spencer a phony because of his obsequious behavior while Mr. Thurber was observing him teach.

4. The man was looking for his initials that he had carved into the bathroom door when he was a student.

5. Holden pictures the nuns holding their straw baskets, collecting money for the poor.

6. James Castle committed suicide rather than "take back" what he said about another student.

7. The only conversation Holden remembers having with James Castle was when James asked to borrow Holden's turtleneck sweater.

8. Phoebe wants Holden to stop swearing.

9. Holden says that he would not know if, as a lawyer, he really wanted to help people or just receive the recognition for helping people.

10. The author is Robert Burns.

Suggested Essay Topics

1. When asked by Phoebe what he likes, Holden can think only of the nuns and James Castle. Why do you suppose he thinks of these people?

2. What do you think is the significance of Holden's wanting to be the catcher in the rye?

Chapter 23

New Character:

Mr. Antolini: *Holden's former English teacher at Elkton Hills*

Summary

It is after 1:00 a.m. when Holden calls Mr. Antolini, who graciously invites him to come over to his apartment right away. Holden returns to the bedroom and dances with Phoebe to four songs on the radio. After they finish, Phoebe hears the front door open. Their parents have returned. Holden quickly hides in the closet. Mrs. Caulfield comes into the bedroom and announces that she saw the light on. Phoebe says that she had trouble sleeping. Her mother then mentions that she smells cigarette smoke. Phoebe covers for Holden by saying that she just took one puff. When her mother leaves the room, Holden comes out of the closet and prepares to leave for Mr. Antolini's. Holden is almost out of money and asks to borrow some money from Phoebe. She gives him all the money that she had saved to buy Christmas presents. This boundless generosity causes Holden to cry, and Phoebe comforts him by putting her arm around him. Holden gives her his hunting hat and leaves the apartment.

Analysis

In this last section of the book (Chapters 21–26), Phoebe becomes the catalyst for Holden's metamorphosis. Phoebe is a child, overflowing with love for Holden, and untouched by the corrupting influences of the world. Her boundless love allows her to tell

him the truth about himself, namely that he is profoundly negative and rejects almost everyone, including himself. When their
mother asks about the smell of smoke in her bedroom, Phoebe
covers for Holden, and says that she lit the cigarette. When Holden
needs money, she gives him all that she has.

Holden is genuinely touched by Phoebe, and he cries. This is
not the first time that Holden has cried, but it is different this time.
These are not tears of anger as before. But he is weeping over himself and his destiny. What has become of him? What is he doing to
his life? Where will he end up? Phoebe is there to comfort him, to
let him know that he is worthwhile, valuable, and deeply loved.
And she does it so simply. She puts her arm around his shoulder
and they draw close together. Phoebe, child that she is, then offers
him the comfort that children want when they are upset: have
someone sleep with them and not have to face the night alone.
This simple love is a rare phenomenon in the world which Holden
is about to enter. He and the reader savor the moment with this
remarkable loving child.

Study Questions

1. How does Mr. Antolini respond to Holden's telephone call?
2. Who taught Phoebe to dance?
3. How does Holden feel after he dances with Phoebe?
4. What behavior of Charlene, the maid, does Phoebe object to?
5. Where does Phoebe say her prayers before she goes to bed that evening?
6. Why does Holden say that he has to leave the house?
7. Why does Phoebe not want Holden to go away?
8. Where does Holden plan to stay until Wednesday?
9. How does Phoebe try to comfort Holden when he is crying?
10. What does Holden do with the hunting hat?

Answers

1. Mr. Antolini responds very graciously, considering that the telephone call is made after 1:00 a.m. Mr. Antolini says that Holden is welcome to come over to his apartment immediately.

2. Holden taught Phoebe how to dance. But he says that she learned it mostly by herself, since you can't teach someone how to really dance.

3. Holden says that he is out of breath because he has been smoking so much. He comments that Phoebe is not out of breath at all.

4. Phoebe says that Charlene breathes all over the food and everything.

5. Phoebe says her prayers in the bathroom that evening.

6. Holden has to leave in order to get his luggage from the train station.

7. Among other reasons, she fears that he will not see her in her play.

8. Holden plans to stay with Mr. Antolini until Wednesday.

9. Phoebe puts her arm around him and then says, in a typically innocent childlike manner, that he can sleep with her if he wants to.

10. Holden gives it to Phoebe as he leaves to visit Mr. Antolini.

Suggested Essay Topics

1. At the end of the chapter, why is it that Holden no longer cares if his parents find him at home?

2. Do you see any significance in the maid, Charlene, breathing on the food and everything?

3. Do you see any symbolism in Phoebe's saying her bedtime prayers in the bathroom?

Chapter 24

New Characters:

Richard Kinsella: *a classmate of Holden's who digressed a great deal in Oral Expression class when giving speeches*

Mr. Vinson: *teacher of Oral Expression at Pencey Prep*

Summary

Holden takes a cab to Mr. Antolini's apartment. It was clear to Holden that Mr. Antolini had been drinking quite a lot that evening, since he and his wife had had a party that evening. Mr. Antolini questioned Holden about his difficulties at Pencey and more specifically how Holden did in his English class. This led to a discussion of Richard Kinsella, a student at Pencey, who was in the same Oral Expression class as Holden. Holden was particularly annoyed with Mr. Vinson, the teacher of the class, because of the way he would interrupt Richard while giving a speech. Although Richard tended to stray from the main topic of his speech, Holden felt that it was rude of Mr. Vinson to be so critical of his digressions. Mr. Antolini tried to defend Mr. Vinson's behavior, but Holden was not interested. Mr. Antolini then lectures Holden on the merits of a good academic education. Holden is visibly tired, and Mr. Antolini realizes that it is time for Holden to go to sleep. They prepare a bed on the couch for Holden, and he quickly falls asleep. Suddenly, Holden is awakened by Mr. Antolini's hand on his head. Holden is frightened by this apparent display of affection and jumps to his feet. As he hurriedly dresses, he makes up an excuse that he has to go to the train station to get his luggage. Mr. Antolini pleads for Holden to go back to bed. Holden, shaken by Mr. Antolini's behavior, leaves the apartment.

Analysis

Antolini is advising Holden not to waste his time or sacrifice his life to some foolish cause. Mr. Antolini recommends rather that he live humbly and simply, according to his beliefs. Antolini says that some men, like Holden, are looking for something that is missing from their lives and should keep looking until they find it. Good advice, indeed, but before you can give yourself to a cause you must believe in something. Some men live humbly for a cause. Some men die nobly for a cause. Some men regrettably just live. But what is it that Holden is willing to die for? What are his beliefs? Mr. Antolini then tells Holden that he sees him dying nobly for some highly unworthy cause. The reader knows that this is not only possible but likely because Holden has no belief system.

Holden is confused and shocked by Mr. Antolini's gesture while he is sleeping. He immediately jumps to the conclusion that Mr. Antolini is making a sexual advance. This is especially disturbing to Holden because Mr. Antolini has been a hero to him. He is also upset because this is not the first time that homosexual advances have been made on him. Perhaps this is true, but one cannot help wondering whether Holden has misinterpreted other attempts by males to get close to him. Holden, still confused and shocked, reflects on this scene in the next chapter.

Study Questions

1. How did Mr. Antolini feel about D.B. going to Hollywood?

2. Why does Mrs. Antolini not want Holden to look at her when she enters the room with the coffee and cake?

3. What criteria does Holden say one must meet in order to get a good grade in Oral Expression?

4. Why does Holden like Richard Kinsella's speeches better than anyone else's?

5. Holden admits that there were times when he hated both Stradlater and Ackley. What else does Holden say about them?

6. What is the sense of the quote from Wilhelm Stekel which Mr. Antolini writes down for Holden?

7. What does Mr. Antolini say that Holden will do once he decides what to do with his life?

8. What does Mr. Antolini say that a good academic education will do for Holden?

9. What excuse does Holden give Mr. Antolini for having to go to the train station to get his money?

10. While awaiting the elevator, what does Holden say to Mr. Antolini?

Answers

1. Mr. Antolini was opposed to D.B. going to Hollywood. He said that anyone who could write as well as D.B. should not go to Hollywood.

2. Mrs. Antolini does not want Holden to look at her because her hair is in curlers and she had removed her makeup.

3. Holden says that to get a good grade in Oral Expression, one must stick to the topic all of the time.

4. Holden finds Richard's speeches exciting because he digresses from his topic and speaks about more interesting subjects.

5. Holden says that, if he did not see them for a period of time, he actually missed both Stradlater and Ackley.

6. The sense of the quote is that the foolish man wants to die for a cause, while the wise man is willing to live for it.

7. Mr. Antolini says that Holden will begin to apply himself in school once he decides what to do with his life.

8. Mr. Antolini says that a good academic education will enable him to express himself more clearly, have a passion for following his thoughts through to the end, and possess more humility than the uneducated man.

9. Holden says that he needs to go to the train station to get his money because it belongs to his mother.

10. Holden tells Mr. Antolini that he is going to read some good books.

Suggested Essay Topics

1. Why do you think Holden was disturbed by Mr. Vinson's behavior toward Richard Kinsella?

2. With regard to Wilhelm Stekel's quote, "The mark of the immature man is that he wants to die nobly for a cause, while

the mark of the mature man is that he wants to live humbly
for one," is everyone who dies for a cause immature? Please
explain. Is there room in this world for both kinds of people?

Chapters 25 and 26

Summary

Holden takes the subway to Grand Central Station and sleeps
there on a bench until 9:00 a.m. He begins to have second thoughts
about whether Mr. Antolini is a homosexual. To distract himself
from these thoughts, Holden reads some magazine articles about
hormones and cancer. In no time at all, Holden begins wondering
whether he has hormone problems and whether he has cancer.
He leaves Grand Central Station and looks for a place to have breakfast. He finds a place, but has only coffee because he is still too
upset about Mr. Antolini to eat. Holden decides again that he will
go out west. He leaves a note for Phoebe at her school, instructing
her to meet him at the museum during her lunch period so he can
say good-bye to her. While waiting for Phoebe, Holden meets two
young boys, who ask him where the mummy exhibit is. Holden
takes them into the tomb, but they get scared and leave him alone.
Leaving the tombs, Holden gets sick with diarrhea, then passes out.
When he comes to, he reports that he no longer feels dizzy, as he
had all morning.

At the appointed time, Phoebe meets him with suitcase in hand
because she wants to go with him. Holden gets angry and makes
her cry. He then tells her that he has decided to go home, not out
west. They both walk to the zoo, but on opposite sides of the street
because Phoebe is pouting. After they look at the sea lions and the
bears, they leave the zoo and walk over to the carousel. Phoebe
stops pouting and begins talking to Holden. He suggests that she
ride the carousel. Before she rides the carousel for the second time,
she places the red hunting hat on his head. It begins to rain. Holden
is overcome with joy as he sits there in the rain, watching Phoebe
ride the carousel.

In the final chapter we find Holden in the psychiatric hospital
from which he has told the story. The logical question is what comes

next? But Holden says that is a stupid question because you do not know what you are going to do until you do it. It is not clear what time of the year it is or for how long he has been in the hospital. It appears that he went into the hospital some time after Christmas, and he is still there well before the beginning of the fall school term. Holden confesses that he still does not understand all that has happened to him. The most he can say is that he misses some of the characters in the story, even ones that he said he did not like.

Analysis

Human maturity usually is understood to mean reason pre-dominating over emotion, i.e., judgments made on the basis of convictions, with a blend of cognition and feeling. Reactive, impulsive decision making, coupled with an inability to see the relationship between short-term and long-term decisions, is characteristic of Holden. For example, Holden impulsively loses his temper with Phoebe and quickly regrets it. After being so sure that Mr. Antolini is a homosexual preying upon him, he begins to wonder whether he has interpreted the situation accurately. But, in both cases, the damage is already done. Secondly, he flunks out of school as a result of a series of failed quizzes, tests, and examinations. He seems to be a prisoner of circumstances and emotions.

In contrast to chance and reactive impulsivity as motivational forces in Holden's life, some readers feel that going home has been the goal of this book from the beginning. Going home seems to symbolize rebirth, getting his life in order, maturity. It has been a circuitous route, but the decision was made in Chapter One.

Much critical attention has been focused on the significance of Holden's hunting hat. The symbolism is effective because, in over 40 years of critical studies of this book, the red hat has been given countless meanings. Some feel that because Holden is conventional in most ways, including his dress, the hat then becomes a statement of rebelliousness. Some writers have seen symbolism in whether he wears the hat forward or backwards. Wearing it backwards, some writers suggest that Holden identifies with a baseball catcher, and on another level, with the catcher in the rye (the protector of children). Wearing it backwards can also suggest that Holden, caught between adulthood and childhood,

wants to regress to childhood where there is goodness and innocence. Wearing it forward, he is now moving into adulthood and
giving up on being the catcher. The hat comes up so often that
some feel it must mean something. Finally, there is a group of
critics, usually with a more cynical bent, who feel that sometimes
hats and cigars are not Freudian symbols, but stand for nothing
more than hats and cigars.

Chapter 26 functions as an epilogue to the book. It
is outside the story. Epilogues usually help explain what went
before, but Salinger leaves this analysis to the reader. Whether
Holden ended up as a Wall Street attorney, working at his father's
firm, or is, in fact, still frequenting Central Park, cursing the absur-
dities of life, nobody knows. Maybe Salinger knows, but he has said
nothing—in over 40 years.

Study Questions

1. Where does Holden spend the rest of the night after he leaves
   Mr. Antolini's apartment?

2. What does Holden worry about as he tries to stop thinking
   about the scene with Mr. Antolini?

3. Whom does Holden think about calling before he meets
   Phoebe?

4. What rule would Holden require all visitors at his cabin to
   observe?

5. How does Holden recognize Phoebe from a distance at the
   museum?

6. Why does Phoebe have a suitcase with her?

7. What does Phoebe say to Holden that he says sounds worse
   than swearing?

8. How does Holden feel as he stands in the rain watching
   Phoebe ride the carousel?

9. From what location is Holden telling this story?

10. What is Holden sorry about?

Answers

1. Holden spends the rest of the night sleeping on a bench in Grand Central Station.

2. Holden begins reading magazine articles about hormones and cancer. He soon begins to worry about his hormones and whether he has cancer.

3. Holden thinks about calling Jane Gallagher, but decides against it because, once again, he is not in the mood.

4. Holden would forbid visitors to do anything phony while they are with him at his cabin.

5. Holden recognizes Phoebe because she is wearing his red hunting hat.

6. Phoebe has a suitcase with her because she wants to go out west with Holden.

7. Phoebe tells him to shut up. This sounds worse than swearing to Holden.

8. Holden says that he feels so happy that he is almost crying.

9. Holden is telling this story from a psychiatric hospital in California.

10. Holden says that he is sorry he told so many people this story.

Suggested Essay Topics

1. References are made to the hunting hat throughout the book. Comment on its symbolism.

2. Holden says that he misses everybody in his story, and he advises the reader never to tell anybody anything, because you start missing everybody. What does this mean?

Sample Analytical Paper Topics

Topic #1

Illustrate how Holden can be viewed as a contemporary Everyman, the main character in a medieval morality play.

Outline

I. Thesis Statement: The Catcher in the Rye *can be viewed as a contemporary morality play.*

II. Historical Context of Morality Play

    A. Definition of morality play

    B. Characteristics of morality play

    C. Morality play (allegory) as a literary genre

III. Everyman

    A. Summary of story

    B. Accidental differences to the stories due to different eras

    C. Lessons *The Catcher in the Rye* teaches us which are similar to Everyman

Topic #2

Discuss symbolism in *The Catcher in the Rye.*

Outline

I. Thesis Statement: *Although much symbolism in* The Catcher in the Rye *is authentic, some critics have argued for symbolism which is illusory at best and trivial at worst.*

II. "Symbols are nothing but the natural speech of drama" (T. Williams).

    A. Words are symbols of concepts.

    B. Symbolic gestures, clothing, etc. can speak more directly and simply than do words.

        1. Gifts of gold, frankincense, and myrrh from the three wise men to Jesus symbolized that Jesus was a king.

        2. White gown of a bride symbolizes her purity.

        3. Wearing a black armband indicates a person in mourning.

        4. A ring on the third finger of the left hand indicates that a person is married.

        5. A military salute

    C. Authentic symbols in *The Catcher in the Rye*

        1. Phoebe and Allie representing innocence and purity

        2. Ducks representing homeless condition of Holden, i.e., evicted from their home by the cold temperature of the environment

        3. Lunatic in the tombs who hurts himself identified with Holden

        4. Holden's passing out in the restroom as a death, and then meeting Phoebe as a resurrection

        5. Breaking of phonograph record as a symbol of the end of childhood

        6. Holden's blowing smoke on the nuns as a sign of his tainting of the innocent

D. Inauthentic or trivial symbols in *The Catcher in the Rye*

1. Holden's falling sensation as he crosses the streets as a falling into adulthood

2. Red hunting hat as a symbol of rebelliousness

3. Prayers in the bathroom suggesting that the bathroom is a sanctuary

4. Holden's frequent use of the term madman symbolizing his own deteriorating mental health

5. The red hunting hat as a consolation prize for failure, i.e., for having left the fencing equipment on the subway

6. Ernie playing the piano in the Greenwich Village nightclub as a symbol of a priest saying mass at the altar

Topic # 3

Many aspects of American life have drastically changed since *The Catcher in the Rye* was first published. Show how Holden's story still has a profound effect on young people today despite these changes.

Outline

I. Thesis Statement: *Even though times have changed drastically, Holden Caulfield speaks as authentically to today's teenagers as he did to his contemporaries over 40 years ago.*

II. How times have changed:

A. *Single-Parent Homes*–There are 8 million single-parent homes today. In 1951, there were relatively few single parent homes.

B. *Working Mothers*–About 50 percent of mothers work outside the home today. In 1951, few mothers worked outside the home. Most of those who did work during the war were either laid off or quit their jobs to provide jobs for men returning from the war.

C. *Sexual Activity*–Over 25 percent of girls are sexually active at age 15. Since birth control methods were limited and not readily accessible, and there was a taboo against bearing children out of wedlock, sexual activity outside of marriage was much less than today.

D. *Violent Crime*–One in six youths between the ages of 10 and 17 has seen or knows someone who has been shot. In 1951, migration of the poor to the cities had just begun, so that violent crime was much less.

E. *Child Abuse*–Reported child abuse has increased two hundred fold since 1950.

F. *Drug and Alcohol Abuse*–Drug and alcohol abuse are enormous social problems today. They were not in 1951.

G. *Mass Communication*–In 1951, every home had one radio, a telephone, and a few had televisions. With communication satellites, faxes, portable phones, and the Internet, the world is truly a global village.

III. Evidence that Holden speaks authentically

A. *The Catcher in the Rye* has remained in print since it was published.

B. The University of Dayton did a survey in late 1994 and found that *The Catcher in the Rye* was the third most popular book to be given for a Christmas gift.

IV. Why teenagers still listen to Holden

A. Holden, although perhaps in an exaggerated manner, speaks of what most teenagers are experiencing, e.g., finding out who you are, what you believe, how life should be lived.

B. The experience of struggling through the teenage years is presented so authentically that young people today can still identify with Holden.

SECTION FOUR

Bibliography

Bloom, Harold, ed. *Holden Caulfield*. New York: Chelsea House Publishers, 1990.

French, Warren. *J.D. Salinger, Revisited*. Boston: Twayne Publishers, Inc., 1988.

——————, *J.D. Salinger*. New York: Twayne Publishers, Inc., 1963.

Green, Martin. *Re-Appraisals: Some Commonsense Readings in American Literature*. New York: W.W. Norton & Company, Inc., 1963.

Grunwald, Henry Anatole, ed. *Salinger: A Critical and Personal Portrait*. New York: Harper & Brothers, 1962.

Gwynn, Frederick and Blotner, Joseph L. *The Fiction of J. D. Salinger*. Pittsburgh: University of Pittsburgh Press, 1958.

Hamilton, Ian. *In Search of J.D. Salinger*. New York: Random House, 1988.

Hamilton, Kenneth. *J.D. Salinger: A Critical Essay*. Wm. B. Eerdmans Publishing Co., 1967.

Laser, Marvin and Fruman, Norman. *Studies in J. D. Salinger: Reviews, Essays, and Critiques of* The Catcher in the Rye *and Other Fiction*. New York: The Odyssey Press, 1963.

Miller, Jr., James E. *J. D. Salinger*. Minneapolis: University of Minnesota Press, 1965.